MW00980079

Divine Conduct Or

The Mystery Of Providence

Wherein The Being And Efficacy Of
Providence Are Asserted And Vindicated The
Methods Of Providence, As It Passes
Through The Several Stages Of Our Lives
Opened And The Proper Course Of
Improving All Providences Pointed Out

John Flavel

Alpha Editions

This Edition Published in 2020

ISBN: 9789354217357

Design and Setting By
Alpha Editions
www.alphaedis.com
Email – info@alphaedis.com

As per information held with us this book is in Public Domain.
This book is a reproduction of an important historical work. Alpha Editions
uses the best technology to reproduce historical work in the same manner
it was first published to preserve its original nature. Any marks or number
seen are left intentionally to preserve its true form.

DIVINE CONDUCT

OR

THE MYSTERY OF PROVIDENCE.

I will cry unto God Most High: unto God that performeth all things for me.—PSALM lvii. 2.

THE greatness of God is a glorious and unsearchable mystery. "The Lord most high is terrible;
he is a great King over all the earth," Psal. xlvii. 2.
The condescension of the most high God to men
is also a profound mystery. "Though the Lord
be high, yet hath he respect unto the lowly,"
Psal. cxxxviii. 6. But when both these meet together, as they do in this Scripture, they make up
a matchless mystery. Here we find the most high
God performing all things for a poor distressed
creature. It is the great support and solace of the
saints in all the distresses that befall them here,
that there is a wise Spirit sitting in all the wheels
of motion, and governing the most eccentric creatures, and their most pernicious designs, to blessed
and happy issues. And, indeed, it were not worth
while to live in a world devoid of God and providence.

How deeply we are concerned in this matter,

3

will appear by that great instance which this psalm presents us with.

It was composed, as the title notes, by David prayer-wise, when he hid himself from Saul in the cave; and is inscribed with a double title, *Al taschith Michtam* of David. *Al taschith* refers to the scope, and *Michtam* to the dignity of the subject-matter.

The former signifies "destroy not," or, let there be no slaughter, and may either refer to Saul, concerning whom he gave charge to his servants not to destroy him; or rather, it hath reference to God, to whom, in this great exigence, he poured out his soul in this pathetical ejaculation, " *Al taschith*, Destroy not !"

The latter title, *Michtam*, signifies a golden ornament, and so is suited to the choice and excellent matter of the psalm, which much more deserves such a title, than Pythagoras's golden verses did.

Three things are remarkable in the former part of the psalm, namely: 1. His extreme danger. 2. His earnest address to God in that extremity. 3. The arguments he pleads with God in that address.

1. His extreme danger, expressed both in the title and body of the psalm. The title tells us, this psalm was composed by him, when he hid himself from Saul, in the cave. This cave was in the wilderness of Engedi, among the broken rocks, where the wild-goats inhabited, an obscure and desolate hole; yet, even thither the envy of Saul pursued him, 1 Sam. xxiv. 1, 2. And now he, that had been so long hunted as a partridge upon the mountains, seems to be inclosed in the net; for the place was begirt with his enemies, and having, in this place, no outlet another way, and

Saul himself entering into the mouth of this cave, in the sides and creeks whereof he and his men lay hid, and saw him, judge to how great an extremity, and to what a desperate state things were now brought; well might he say, as it is, ver. 4. "My soul is among lions, and I lie even among them that are set on fire." What hope now remained? what but immediate destruction could be expected?

2. Yet this frights him not out of his faith and duty, but between the jaws of death he prays, and earnestly addresses himself to God for mercy: "Be merciful unto me, O God, be merciful unto me," ver. 1. This excellent psalm was composed by him when there was enough to discompose the best man in the world. The repetition denotes both the extremity of the danger, and the ardency of the supplicant. Mercy, mercy! nothing but mercy, and that exerting itself in an extraordinary way, can now save him from ruin.

3. The arguments he pleads for obtaining mercy, in this distress, are very considerable.

(1.) He pleads his reliance upon God as an argument to move mercy; "Be merciful unto me, O God, be merciful unto me; for my soul trusteth in thee; yea, in the shadow of thy wings will I make my refuge, until these calamities be overpast," ver. 1. This his trust and dependence on God, though it be not argumentative in respect of the dignity of the act, yet is so in respect both of the nature of the object, a compassionate God, who will not expose any that take shelter under his wings; and in respect of the promise, whereby protection is assured to them that fly to him for sanctuary; "Thou wilt keep him in perfect peace, whose mind is stayed on thee, because he trusteth

1 *

in thee," Isa. xxvi. 3. Thus he encourages himself from the consideration of that God to whom
he betakes himself.

(2.) He pleads former experiences of his help,
in past distresses, as an argument, encouraging
hope under the present strait. "I will cry unto
God most high: unto God that performeth all
things for me," ver. 2. In which words, I shall
consider two things, 1. The duty resolved upon.
2. The encouragement to that resolution. 1. The
duty resolved upon: "I will cry unto God."
Crying unto God is an expression that doth not
only denote prayer, but intense and fervent prayer.
To cry is to pray in a holy passion; and such
are usually speeding prayers, Psal. xviii. 6, and Heb.
v. 7. 2. The encouragements to this resolution;
and these are two-fold. (1.) Objective, taken from
the sovereignty of God. (2.) Subjective, taken
from the experience he had of his providence.
(1.) The sovereignty of God: "I will cry unto
God most high." Upon this he acts his faith in
extremity of danger. Saul is high, but God the
most high; and, without his permission, he is
assured Saul cannot touch him. He had none to
help; and if he had, he knew God must first help
the helpers, or they cannot help him. He had no
means of defence or escape before him, but the
Most High is not limited by means. This is a
singular prop to faith, Psal. lix. 9. (2.) The experience of his providence hitherto: "Unto God
that performeth all things for me." The word
which we translate *performeth*, comes from a root,
that signifies both to perfect, and to desist, or cease.
For when a business is performed and perfected,
the agent then ceases and desists from working;
he puts to the last hand, when he finishes the

work. To such a happy issue the Lord hath brought all his doubtful and difficult matters before; and this gives him encouragement, that he will still be gracious, and perfect that which concerneth him now, as he speaks: "The Lord will perfect that which concerneth me," Psal. cxxxviii. 8. The Septuagint renders it, "who profiteth, or benefitteth me." And it is a certain truth, that all the results and issues of Providence are profitable and beneficial to the saints. But the supplement in our translation well receives the importance of the place, "who performeth all things," and involves the most strict and proper notion of Providence, which is nothing else but the performance of God's gracious purposes and promises to his people. And therefore Vatablus and Muis supply and fill up the room, which the conciseness of the original leaves, thus, "I will cry unto God most high: unto God that performeth the things which he hath promised." Payment is the performance of promises. Grace makes the promise, and providence the payment.

Piscator fills it with, "Unto God that performeth his kindness and mercy." But still it supposes the mercy performed to be contained in the promise. Mercy is sweet in the promise, and much more so in the providential performance of it to us.

Castalio's supplement comes nearer to ours: "I will cry unto God most high, unto God the transactor of my affairs."

But our English, making out the sense by a universal particle, is most fully agreeable to the scope of the text. For it cannot but be a great encouragement to his faith, that God hath transacted all things, or performed all things for him. This Providence, that never failed him in any of

the straits that ever he met with, (and his life was
a life of many straits,) he might well hope, would
not now fail him, though this were an extraordinary and matchless one.

Bring we, then, our thoughts a little closer to
this Scripture, and it will give us a fair and lovely
prospect of Providence.

In its 1. Universal, 2. Effectual, 3. Beneficial,
4. Encouraging influences upon the affairs and
concerns of the saints.

(1.) The expression imports the universal interest and influence of Providence in and upon all
the concerns and interests of the saints. It hath
not only its hand in this or that, but in all that
concerns them. It hath its eye upon every thing
that relates to them throughout their lives, from
first to last. Not only great and more important,
but the most minute and ordinary affairs of our
lives are transacted and managed by it. It touches
all things that touch us, whether more nearly or
remotely.

(2.) It displays the efficacy of providential influences. Providence doth not only undertake,
but performs and perfects what concerns us. It
goes through with its designs, and accomplishes
what it begins. No difficulty so clogs it, no cross
accident so falls in its way, but it carries its design
through it. Its motions are irresistible and uncon-
trollable; he performs it for us.

(3.) And, which is sweet to consider, all its
products and issues are exceedingly beneficial to
the saints. It performs all things for them. It is
true, we often prejudice its works, and unjustly
censure its designs, and, under many of our straits
and troubles, we say, "All these things are against
us." But indeed Providence neither doth nor can

do any thing that is really against the true interest and good of the saints. For what are the works of Providence but the execution of God's decree, and the fulfilling of his word? and there can be no more in Providence than is in them. Now there is nothing but good to the saints in God's purposes and promises; and, therefore, whatever Providence doth in their concerns, it must be, as the text speaks, "the performance of all things for them."

(4.) And if so, how cheering, supporting, and encouraging must the consideration of these things be in a day of distress and trouble! What life and hope will it inspire our hearts and prayers with, when great pressures lie upon us! It had such a cheering influence upon the psalmist at this time, when the state of his affairs was, to the eye of sense and reason, forlorn and desperate. There was then but a hair's breadth, as we say, between him and ruin.

A potent, enraged, and implacable enemy had driven him into the hole of a rock, and was come after him into that hole; yet now, whilst " his soul is among lions," whilst he lies in a cranny of the rock, expecting every moment to be drawn out to death, the reflections he had upon the gracious performances of the Most High for him, from the beginning to that moment, supported his soul, and inspired hope and life into his prayers: "I will cry unto God most high: unto God that performeth all things for me."

The amount of all, you have in this doctrinal conclusion:

That it is the duty of the saints, especially in times of straits, to reflect upon the performances

*of Providence for them, in all the states, and
through all the stages of their lives.*

The church, in all the works of mercy, owns the
hand of God: "Lord, thou hast wrought all our
works in" or for "us," Isa. xxvi. 12. And still
it hath been the pious and constant practice of the
saints, in all generations, to preserve the memory
of the more famous and remarkable providences
that have befallen them in their times, as a precious treasure. If thou be a Christian indeed, I
know thou hast, if not in thy book, yet certainly
in thy heart, a great many precious favours upon
record. The very remembrance and rehearsal of
them is sweet; how much more sweet was the
actual enjoyment! Thus Moses, by Divine direction, wrote a memorial of that victory obtained
over Amalek, as the fruit and return of prayer,
and built there an altar, with this inscription,
Jehovah-Nissi, "The Lord my banner," Exod.
xvii. 14, 15. Thus Mordecai and Esther took all
care to perpetuate the memory of that signal deliverance from the plot of Haman, by ordaining the
feast of Purim, as an anniversary throughout every
generation, every family, every province, and
every city, that those days of Purim should not
fail from among the Jews, nor the memorial of
them perish from their seed, Esther ix. 28. For
this end you find psalms indited, "To bring to
remembrance," Psal. lxx. the title; parents giving
suitable names to their children, that every time
they looked upon them they might refresh the
memory of God's mercies, 1 Sam. i. 20; the very
places, where eminent providences have appeared,
new named upon no other design but to perpetuate
the memorial of those sweet providences which so

refresh them there : thence Bethel took its name, Gen. xxviii. 19 ; and that well of water where Hagar was seasonably refreshed by the angel in her distress, Beer-lahai-roi, " the well of him that liveth and looketh on me," Gen. xvi. 14. Yea, the saints have given, and God hath assumed to himself, new titles upon this very score and account : Abraham's Jehovah-jireh, The Lord will provide, and Gideon's Jehovah-shallum, The Lord send peace, were ascribed to him upon this reason. And sometimes you find the Lord style himself, The God that brought Abraham from Ur of the Chaldees ; then the Lord God that brought them out of Egypt ; then The Lord that gathered them out of the north country ; still minding them of the gracious providences which in all those places he had wrought for them.

Now there is a twofold reflection upon the providential works of God. 1. One entire and full, in the whole complex and perfect frame thereof. This blessed sight is reserved for the perfect state.* It is in that mount of God where we shall see both the wilderness and Canaan ; the glorious kingdom into which we are to come, and the way through which we were led into it. There the saints shall have a ravishing view of that beautiful frame; and every part shall be distinctly discerned, as if it had its particular use, and it was connected with the other parts, and how effectually and orderly they

* When the records of eternity shall be exposed to view; all the counsels and results of the profound wisdom looked into, how will it transport! when it shall be discerned, Lo! thus were the designs laid! here were the apt junctures and admirable dependencies of things, which, when acted upon the stage of time, seemed so perplexed and intricate. *Howe's Blessedness,* p. 76.

all wrought to bring about that blessed design of their salvation, according to the promise, " And we know that all things work together for good to them that love God," &c. Rom. viii. 28. For it is certain that no ship at sea keeps more exactly by the compass which directs its course, than Providence doth by that promise which is its pole-star. 2. The other, partial and imperfect in the way to glory, where we only view it in its simple acts, or, at most, in some branches and more observable course of actions.

Between these two is the same difference as between the sight of the disjointed wheels and scattered pins of a watch, and the sight of the whole, united in one frame, and working in one orderly motion; or between an ignorant spectator's viewing some more observable vessel or joint of a dissected body, and the accurate anatomist's discerning the course of all the veins and arteries of the body, as he follows the several branches of them through the whole, and plainly sees the proper places, figure, and use of each, with their mutual respect to one another.

Oh how ravishing and delightful a sight is that! to behold at one view the whole design of Providence, and the proper place and use of every single act which we could not understand in this world! For, what Christ said to Peter, John xiii. 7, is as applicable to some providences in which we are now concerned, as it was to that particular action: " What I do thou knowest not now, but thou shalt know hereafter." All the dark, intricate, puzzling providences, at which we were sometimes so stumbled, and sometimes amazed, which we could neither reconcile with the promise nor with each other; nay, which we so unjustly censured and bitterly bewailed, as if they had fallen out quite cross to our happiness, we shall then see to be unto us, as the difficult passage through the wilderness was unto Israel, " The right way to a city of habitation," Psal. cvii. 7.

And yet, though our present views and reflections upon Providence be so short and imperfect, in comparison with that in heaven, yet such as it is, under all its present disadvantages, it hath so much excellency and sweetness in it, that I may call it a little heaven, or, as Jacob called his Bethel, The gate of heaven. It is certainly a highway of walking with God in this world, and as sweet communion may a soul enjoy with him in his providences as in any of his ordinances. How often have the hearts of its observers been melted into tears of joy at the beholding of its wise and unexpected productions ! How often hath it convinced them, upon a sober recollection of the events of their lives, that if the Lord had left them to their own counsels, they had as often been their own tormentors, if not executioners ! Into what and how many fatal mischiefs had they precipitated themselves, if Providence had been as short-sighted as they. They have given it their hearty thanks for considering their interest more than their importunity, and not suffering them to perish by their own desires.

The benefits of adverting to the works of Providence are manifold and unspeakable, as, in its place, we shall show you. But not to entangle the thread of the discourse, I shall cast it into this method :

First. I shall prove that the concerns of the saints, in this world, are certainly conducted by the wisdom and care of special Providence.

2

Second. I will show you in what particular concerns of theirs this providential care is evidently discovered.

Third. That it is the duty of saints to advert to, and carefully observe these performances of Providence for them in all their concernments.

Fourth. In what manner this duty is to be performed by them.

Fifth. What singular benefits result to them from such observations; and then apply the whole in such uses as offer themselves from the point.

THE FIRST GENERAL HEAD.

First. I shall undertake the proof and defence of this great truth: "That the affairs of the saints in this world are certainly conducted by the wisdom and care of special Providence."

And herein I address myself with cheerfulness to perform, as well as I am able, a service for that Providence, which hath, throughout my life, " performed all things for me," as the text speaks.

There is a twofold consideration of Providence, according to its twofold object and manner of dispensation: the one is general, exercised about all creatures, rational and irrational, animate and inanimate; the other special and peculiar. Christ hath a universal empire over all things, Ephes. i. 22, the head of the whole world, by way of dominion; but a head to the Church, by way of union and special influence, John xvii. 2. "The Saviour of all men, but especially of them that believe," 1 Tim. iv. 10. The Church is his special care and charge; he rules the world for her good, as a head consulting the welfare of the body.

Heathens generally deny providence; and no wonder, since they denied a God: for the same

arguments that prove one, will prove the other.
Aristotle, the prince of heathen philosophers, could
not, by the utmost search of reason, find out the
world's origin, and therefore concludes, it was
from eternity. The Epicureans did, in a sort,
acknowledge a God, but yet denied a providence,
and wholly excluded him from any interest or concern in the affairs of the world, as being incon-
sistent with the felicity and tranquillity of the
Divine Being, to be diverted and cumbered with
the care and labour of government. This asser-
tion is so repugnant to reason, that it is a wonder
they themselves blushed not at its absurdity; but
I guess at the design, and one of them speaks it
out in broad language. They foresaw that the
concession of a providence would impose an eternal yoke upon their necks, by making them ac-
countable to a higher tribunal for all they did; and
that they must necessarily pass the time of their
sojourning here in fear, whilst all their thoughts,
words, and ways, were strictly noted and recorded, in order to an account, by an all-seeing and
righteous God; and therefore they laboured to
persuade themselves that that was not, which they had
no mind should be. But these atheistical and
foolish conceits fall flat before the undeniable evidence of so great and clear a truth.

Now my business here is not so much to deal
with professed atheists, who deny the existence of
God, and consequently deride all evidences brought
from Scripture, of the extraordinary events that fall
out in favour of that people who are called his; but
rather to convince those who professedly own all
this, yet, never having tasted religion by experience, suspect, at least, that all these things which
we call special providences to the saints, are but

natural events, or mere contingencies; and thus,
whilst they profess to own a God and a providence,
(which profession is but the effect of their education,) they do, in the mean time, live like atheists,
and both think and act as if there were no such
things; and really I fear this is the case of the far
greatest part of men of this generation.

But if it were indeed so, that the affairs of the
world, in general, and more especially those of the
saints, were not conducted by divine Providence,
but, as they would persuade us, by the steady
course of natural causes; besides which, if at any
time we observe an event to fall out, it is merely
casual and contingent, or that which proceeds from
some hidden and secret cause in nature; if this indeed were so, let those who are tempted to believe
it, rationally satisfy the following demands:

First demand. How comes it to pass that so
many signal mercies and deliverances have befallen the people of God, above the power and
against the course of natural causes; to make way
for which, there hath been a sensible suspension
and stop put to the course of nature? It is most
evident that no natural effect can exceed the power
of its natural cause. Nothing can give to another
more than it hath in itself; and it is as clear, that
whatsoever acts naturally, acts necessarily. Fire
burns to the utmost of its power; waters overflow
and drown all that they can. Lions, and other
rapacious and cruel beasts, tear and devour their
prey, especially when hungry; and as to arbitrary
and rational agents, they also act according to the
principles and laws of their natures. A wicked
man, when his heart is fully set in him, and his
will stands in a full bent of resolution, will certainly,
if he have power in his hand, and opportunity

to execute his conceived mischief, give it vent, and
perpetrate the wicked devices of his heart; for,
having once conceived mischief, and travailing in
pain with it, he must, according to the course of nature, bring it forth, as it is in Psal. vii. 14. But if
any of these inanimate, brutal, or rational agents,
when there is no natural obstacle, have their power
suspended; and that when the effect is near the
birth, and the design, at the very article of execution,
so that though they would, yet they cannot hurt; to
what, think you, is this to be assigned and refer-
red? Yet so it hath often been seen, where God's
interest hath been immediately concerned in the
danger and evil of the event. The sea divided itself in its own channel, and made a wall of water
on each side, to give God's distressed Israel a safe
passage, and that not in a calm, but, " when the
waves thereof roared,"* as it is in Isa. li. 15. The
fire when blown up to the most intense and vehement flame, had no power to singe one hair of
God's faithful witnesses, when, at the same instant
it had power to destroy their intended executioners at a greater distance, Dan. iii. 22. Yea, we
find it hath been sometimes sufficient to consume,
but not to torment the body, as in that known instance of blessed Byneham, who told his enemies
the flames were to him as a bed of roses. The
hungry lions put off their natural fierceness, and
became gentle and harmless, when Daniel was cast
among them for a prey. The like account, the

* How hard was Porphyry put to it, when, instead
of a better, this pretence must serve the turn: That
Moses taking the advantage of a low water unknown
to the Egyptians, passed over the people thereat; as if
Moses, a stranger, were better acquainted there than
the Egyptian natives.

2*

church history gives us of Polycarp and Dionysius
Areopagita, whom the fire would not touch, but
stood after the manner of a ship's sail, filled with
the wind about them.

Are these things according to the course and law
of nature? To what secret natural cause can they
be ascribed? In like manner, we find the vilest
and fiercest of wicked men have been withheld,
by an invisible hand of restraint, from injuring the
Lord's people. By what secret cause in nature
was Jeroboam's hand dried up, and made inflexi-
ble at the same instant it was stretched out against
the man of God? 1 Kings xiii. 4. No wild beasts
rend and devour their prey more greedily than
wicked men would destroy the people of God who
dwell among them, were it not for this providential
restraint upon them. So the psalmist expresses
his case in the words following my text: "My
soul is among lions, and I lie among them that are
set on fire." The disciples were sent forth as
sheep into the midst of wolves, Matt. x. 16. It
will not avail, in this case, to object by saying that
those miraculous events depend only upon Scripture testimony, which is not assented to by the
atheist: for, besides all that may be alleged for the
authority of that testimony, (which is needless to
produce to men that own it,) what is it less than
every eye sees or may see at this day? Do we not
behold a weak, defenceless handful of men, wonderfully and, except this way, unaccountably preserved from ruin in the midst of potent, enraged,
and turbulent enemies, that fain would, but cannot destroy them, when as yet no natural impediment can
be assigned why they cannot?

And if this puzzle us, what shall we say when
we see events produced in the world, for the good

of God's chosen, by those very hands and means which were intentionally employed for their ruin? These things are as much beside the intentions of their enemies, as they are above their own expectations; yet such things are no rarities in the world. Were not the envy of Joseph's brethren, the cursed plot of Haman, the decree procured by the envy of the princes against Daniel, with many more of the like nature, all turned, by a secret and strange hand of Providence, to their greater advancement and benefit? Their enemies lifted them up to all that honour and preferment they had.

Second demand. How is it, if the saints' concerns are not ordered by a special Divine Providence, that natural causes unite and associate themselves for their relief and benefit in so strange a manner as they are found to do? It is undeniably evident, that there are marvellous coincidences of Providence confederating and agreeing, as it were, to meet and unite themselves to bring about the good of God's chosen. There is a like face of things, showing itself in divers places at that time when any work, for the good of the church, is come upon the stage of the world; as when the Messiah, the capital mercy, came to the temple, then Simeon and Anna were brought thither, by Providence, as witnesses to it : so, in the reformation work, when the images were pulled down in Holland, one and the same spirit of zeal possessed them in every city and town, that the work was done in the night. He that carefully reads the history of Joseph's advancement to be the lord of Egypt, may number in that history twelve remarkable acts or steps of Providence, by which he ascended to that honour and authority; if but one of them had failed, in all likelihood the event had done so too; but every one fell in its order, exactly keeping its own time and place. So, in the church's deliverance from the plot of Haman, we find no less than seven acts of Providence strangely concurring to produce it, as if they had all met by appointment and consent, to break that snare for them; one thing so aptly suiting with and making way for another, that every careful observer must needs conclude this cannot be the effect of casualty, but wise counsel. Even as in viewing the accurate structure of the body of a man, the figure, position, and mutual respects of the several members and vessels have convinced some, and are sufficient to convince all, that it was the effect of Divine wisdom and power; in like manner, if the admirable adapting of the means and instruments employed for mercy to the people of God be heedfully considered, who can fail to confess, that as there are tools of all sorts and sizes in the shop of Providence, so there is a most skilful hand that uses them; and that they could no more produce such effects of themselves, than the axe, saw, or chisel, can cut or carve a rude log into a beautiful figure without the hand of a skilful artificer.

We find, by manifold instances, that there certainly are strong combinations and predispositions of persons and things, to bring about some issue and design for the benefit of the church, which they themselves never thought of. They hold no intelligence, communicate not their counsels to each other, yet meet together, and work together, as if they did; which is as if ten men should all meet together at one place, and in one hour, about one and the same business, and that without any fore-appointment among themselves. Can any question that such a meeting of means and instruments, is certainly, though secretly, overruled by some wise invisible Agent?

Third demand. If the concerns of God's people be not governed by a special Providence, whence is it that the most apt and powerful means, employed to destroy them, are rendered ineffectual; and weak, contemptible means, employed for their defence and comfort, crowned with success? This could never be, if things were wholly swayed by the course of nature. If we judge by that rule, we must conclude, the more apt and powerful the means are, the more successful and prosperous they must needs be; and where they are unfit, weak, and contemptible, nothing can be expected from them. Thus, reason lays it according to the rules of nature; but Providence crosses its hands, as Jacob did in blessing the sons of Joseph, and orders quite contrary issues and events. Such was the mighty power and deep policy used by Pharaoh to destroy God's Israel, that, to the eye of reason, it was as impossible to survive it, as for crackling thorns to abide unconsumed amidst devouring flames; by which emblem, their miraculous preservation is expressed, Exod. iii. 2; the bush was all in a flame, but no consumption of it. The heathen Roman emperors, who made the world tremble, and subdued the nations under them, have employed all their power and policy against the poor, naked, defenceless church, to ruin it, yet could not accomplish it, Rev. xii. 3, 4. Oh, the seas of blood that heathen Rome shed in ten persecutions! yet, the church lives; and, when the dragon gave his power to the beast, Rev. xiii. 2, that is, the state of Rome became anti-christian, oh what slaughters were made by the beast in all his dominions! so that the Holy Ghost represents him as drunken

with the blood of the saints, Rev. xvii. 6. And
yet all will not do ; the gates, that is, the powers and
policies of hell, cannot prevail against it. How
manifest is the care and power of Providence herein ! Had half that power been employed against
any other people, it had certainly swallowed them
up immediately, or, in the hundredth part of the
time, worn them out. How soon was the Persian
monarchy swallowed up by the Grecian, and that
again by the Roman ! Dioclesian and Maximinus,
in the height of their persecution, found themselves
so baffled by Providence, that they both resigned
the government, and lived as private men. But,
in this wonderful preservation, God makes good
that promise, " Though I make a full end of all
nations, yet will I not make a full end of thee,"
Jer. xxx. 11. And again, " No weapon formed
against thee shall prosper," Isa. liv. 17. On the
contrary, how successful have weak and contemptible means been made for the good of the church !
Thus, in the first planting of Christianity in the
world, by what weak, contemptible instruments was
it done ! Christ did not choose the eloquent orators,
or men of authority in the courts of kings and emperors, but twelve poor mechanics and fishermen; and these not sent together in a troop, but
some to take one country to conquer it, and some
another ; the most ridiculous course, in appearance,
for such a design as could be imagined ; and yet,
in how short a time was the gospel spread, and the
churches planted by them in the several kingdoms
of the world ! This the psalmist foresaw by the
spirit of prophecy, when he said, " Out of the mouth
of babes and sucklings hast thou ordained strength,
that thou mightest still the enemy and the aven-
ger," Psal. viii. 2. At the sound of rams' horns

Jericho is delivered into the hands of Israel; see Josh. vi. 20. By three hundred men, with their pitchers and lamps, the huge host of Midian is discomfited, Judges vii. 19. The Protestants besieged at Beziers in France, are delivered by a drunken drummer, who, going to his quarters at midnight, rang the alarm bell of the town, not knowing what he did, and just then their enemies were making their assault. And, as weak and improbable means have been blessed with success to the church in general, so, to the preservation of its particular members also. A spider, by weaving her web over the mouth of an oven, shall hide a servant of Christ, (Du Moulin) from his enemies, who took refuge there in the bloody Parisian massacre. A hen shall sustain another many days at the same time, by lodging her egg every day in the place where he had hid himself from the cutthroats. Examples might be easily multiplied in the case; but the truth is too plain and obvious to the observation of all ages to need them. And can we fail to acknowledge a Divine and special Providence overruling these matters, when we see the most apt and potent means for the church's ruin frustrated, and the most silly and contemptible means succeeded and prospered for its good?

Fourth demand. If all things be governed by the course of natural causes, how then comes it to pass that men are turned, like a bowl by a rub,* out of the way of evil, unto which they were driving on with full speed? Good men have been engaged in the way to their own ruin, and knew it not; but Providence hath met them in the way and preserved them by strange diversions, tho

---

* Hinderance, obstruction, difficulty.

meaning of which they understood not until the
event discovered it. Paul lay bound at Cesarea ;
the high-priest and chief of the Jews request Fes-
tus, that he might be brought bound to Jerusalem,
having laid wait in the way to kill him: but Fes-
tus, though ignorant of the plot, utterly refuses it,
but chooses rather to go with them to Cesarea, and
judge him there. By this check, their bloody design
is frustrated, Acts xxv. 3, 4.

Posidonius, in the life of Augustine, tells us
that the good father going to teach the people of a
certain town, took a guide with him to show him
the way. The guide mistook the usual road, and
ignorantly fell into a by-path, by which means he
escaped ruin by the hands of the bloody Donatists,
who, knowing his intention, way-laid him to kill
him in the road.

And as memorable and wonderful are those checks
and diversions which wicked men have met with
in the way of perpetrating the evils conceived and
intended in their own hearts. Laban and Esau
came against Jacob with mischievous purposes,
Gen. xxxi. 24, but no sooner are they come nigh
to him, than the shackles of restraint are immediately clapt upon them both, so that their hands
cannot perform their enterprises. Balaam runs
greedily for reward to curse Israel, but meets with
an unexpected check at his very outset; and
though that stopped him not, but he tried every
way to do them mischief, yet he still finds himself
fettered by an effectual bond of restraint that he
can no way shake off, Numb. xxii. 25–38. Saul,
the high-priest's blood-hound, breathes out threatenings against the church, and goes, with a bloody
commission, towards Damascus, to hale the poor
flock of Christ to the slaughter; but when he

comes nigh to the place, he meets an unexpected stop in the way, by which the mischief is not only diverted, but himself converted to Christ, Acts ix. 1–4. Who can fail to see the finger of God in these things?

Fifth demand. If there be not an overruling Providence, ordering all things for the good of God's people, how comes it to pass that the good and evil which is done to them in this world is accordingly repaid into the bosom of those who are instrumental therein?

1. How clear is it to every man's observation, that the kindnesses and benefits any have done to the Lord's people have been rewarded with full measure into their bosoms! The Egyptian midwives refused to obey Pharaoh's inhuman command, and saved the male children of Israel; for this the Lord dealt with them, and built them houses, Exod. i. 21. The Shunammite was hospitable, and careful for Elisha, and God recompensed it with the desirable enjoyment of a son, 2 Kings iv. 9, 17. Rahab hid the spies, and was exempted from the common destruction for it, Heb. xi. 31. Publius, the chief man of the island of Melita, courteously received and lodged Paul after his shipwreck. The Lord speedily repaid him for that kindness, and healed his father, who lay sick at that time of a bloody flux and fever, Acts xxviii. 7, 8.

In like manner, we find the evils done to God's people have been repaid by a just retribution to their enemies.

Pharaoh and the Egyptians were cruel enemies to God's Israel, and designed the ruin of their poor innocent babes; and God repaid it by smiting all the first-born in Egypt in one night, Exod. xii. 29.

Haman erected a gallows fifty cubits high for
good Mordecai; and God so ordered it, that he
himself and his ten sons were hanged on it.   And
indeed it was but meet that he should eat the fruit
of that tree which he himself had planted, Esther
vii. 10.

Ahithophel plots against David, and gives counsel, like an oracle, how to procure his fall; and
that very counsel, like a surcharged gun, recoils
upon himself, and procures his ruin; for, seeing
his good counsel rejected, (good *politically*, not
morally,) it was now easy for him to guess at the
issue, and so at his own fate, 2 Sam. xvii. 2, 3.

Charles IX. most inhumanly made the very
canals of Paris to stream with Protestant blood,
and soon after, he died miserably, his blood stream-
ing from all parts of his body.

Stephen Gardiner, who burnt so many of God's
dear servants to ashes, was himself so scorched up
by a terrible inflammation, that his very tongue
was black, and hung out of his mouth; and in
dreadful torments he ended his wretched days.

Maximinus, that cruel emperor, who set forth his
proclamation, engraven in brass, for the utter abo-
lishing of the Christian religion, was speedily smitten, like Herod, with a dreadful judgment, swarms
of lice preying upon his entrails, and causing such
a stench, that his physicians could not endure to
come nigh him, and for refusing it were slain.
Hundreds of like instances might easily be produced to confirm this observation.   And who can fail
to see by these things, that " verily there is a God
that judgeth in the earth ?"

Yea, so exact have been the retributions of Providence to the enemies of the Church, that not
only the same persons, but the same members,

that have been the instruments of mischief, have been made the subjects of wrath.

The same arm, which Jeroboam stretched out to smite the prophet, God smites. The emperor Aurelian, when he was ready to subscribe the edict for the persecution of the Christians, was suddenly cramped in his knuckles that he could not write.

Mr. Greenhill, in his exposition upon Ezekiel xi. 13, tells his auditory, that there was one then present in the congregation, who was an eye-witness of a woman scoffing at another for purity and holy walking, who had her tongue stricken immediately with the palsy, and died thereof within two days.

Henry II. of France, in a great rage against a Protestant counsellor, committed him into the hands of one of his nobles to be imprisoned, and that with these words, that he would see him burnt with his own eyes. But mark the righteous providence of God : within a few days after, the same nobleman, with a lance put into his hands by the king, did, at a tilting match, run the said lance into one of the king's eyes, whereof he died.

Yea, Providence hath made the very place of sinning the place of punishment: " In the place where dogs licked the blood of Naboth, shall dogs lick thy blood," 1 Kings xxi. 19, and it was exactly fulfilled, 2 Kings ix. 26. Thus Tophet is made a burying-place for the Jews, until there is no room to bury; and that was the place where they had offered up their sons to Moloch, Jer. vi. 31, 32. The story of Nightingale is generally known, which Mr. Fox relates, how he fell out of

the pulpit and broke his neck, whilst he was abus-
ing that Scripture, 1 John i. 10.

And thus the Scriptures are made good by Providence: " Whoso diggeth a pit, shall fall therein ;
and he that rolleth a stone, it shall return upon
him," Prov. xxvi. 27 ; and " with what measure
ye mete, it shall be measured to you again,"
Matt. vii. 2.

If any yet say, These things may fall out casually, that many thousands of the enemies of the
Church have died in peace, and their end been like
other men : we answer with Augustine, if no sin
were punished here, no providence would be believed ; and if every sin should be punished here,
no judgment would be expected. But, that none
may think these events to be merely casual and
accidental we yet further demand.

Sixth demand. If these things be merely casual,
how is it that they square and agree so exactly
with the Scriptures in all particulars ?

We read, " Can two walk together, except they
be agreed?" Amos iii. 3. If two men travel in one
road, it is likely they are agreed to go to the same
place. Providences and Scriptures go all one way;
and if they seem at any time to go divers or contrary ways, be sure they will meet at the journey's
end. There is an agreement between them so
to do.

Doth God miraculously suspend the power of
natural causes, as in the first demand was opened?
Why, this is no accidental thing, but what har-
monizes with the word : " When thou passest
through the waters, I will be with thee ; and
through the rivers, they shall not overflow thee.
When thou walkest through the fire, thou shalt

not be burnt, neither shall the flame kindle upon thee," Isaiah xliii. 2.

Do natural causes unite and associate themselves for the good of God's people? Why, this is no more than what is contained in the promises, and is but the fulfilling of that Scripture, " all is yours, for ye are Christ's," 1 Cor. iii. 22 ; that is, the use, benefit, and service of all the creatures are for you, as your need shall require.

Are the most apt and powerful means employed for their ruin, frustrated? Who can but see the Scriptures fulfilled in, and expounded by, such providences? See Isa. xlv. 15–17, and Isa. viii. 7–10, expounded by 2 Kings xviii. 17, &c.

See you at any time a check of Providence divert-ing the course of good men from falling into evil, or wicked men from committing evil? How loud-ly do such providences proclaim the truth and cer-tainty of the Scriptures, which tell us, " that the way of man is not in himself, neither is it in him that walks to direct his steps," Jer. x. 23; and that " a man's heart deviseth his way, but the Lord directeth his steps," Prov. xvi. 9.

Do you see adequate retributions made to those that injure or befriend the people of God? When you see all the kindness and love any have shown the saints returned with an overplus into their bo-soms, how is it possible but you must see the accomplishment of those Scriptures in such provi-dences? " The liberal soul deviseth liberal things, and by liberal things he shall stand," Isa. xxxii. 8, and 2 Cor. ix. 6. And when you see the evils men have done, or intended to do, to the Lord's people, recoiling upon themselves, he is perfectly blind who sees not the harmony such providences

3*

bear with these Scriptures, Psal. cxl. 11, 12 ; vii. 14–16 ; ix. 16.

Oh what exact proportions do providences and Scriptures hold ! Little do men take notice of it. Why did Cyrus, contrary to all rules of state policy, freely dismiss the captives, but to fulfil that Scripture, Isa. xlv. 13 ? So that it was well observed by one, That as God had stretched out the firmament over the natural, so he hath stretched out his word over the rational world ; and as the creatures on earth are influenced by those heavenly bodies, so are all creatures in the world influenced by the word, and do infallibly fulfil it when they design to cross it.

Seventh demand. If these things be contingent, how is it that they fall out in such remarkable nicks and junctures of time, which makes them so greatly observable to all that consider them ?

We find a multitude of providences so timed to a minute, that, had they fallen out ever so little sooner or later, they had signified but little to what they now do. Certainly it cannot be casualty, but counsel, that so exactly nicks the opportunity. Contingencies keep to no rules.

How remarkable to this purpose were the tidings brought to Saul, that the Philistines had invaded the land, just as he was ready to grasp the prey ! 1 Sam. xxiii. 27. The angel calls to Abraham, and shows him another sacrifice, just when his hand was giving the fatal stroke to Isaac. Gen. xxii. 10, 11. A well of water is discovered to Hagar just when she had left the child as not able to see its death, Gen. xxi. 16, 19. Rabshakeh meets with a blasting providence, hears a rumour that frustrated his design, just when ready to give

the shock against Jerusalem, Isa. xxxvii. 7, 8.
So when Haman's plot against the Jews was ripe,
and all things ready for execution, " on that night
could not the king sleep," Esther vi. 1. When
the horns are ready to gore Judah, immediately
carpenters are prepared to drive them away, Zech.
i. 18–21. How remarkable was the relief of
Rochelle, by a shoal of fish that came into the
harbour when they were ready to perish with
famine, such as they never observed before or
after that time. Mr. Dodd could not go to bed one
night, but had a strong impulse to visit, (though
unseasonable,) a neighbouring gentleman, and just
as he came, he meets him at his door, with a halter in his pocket, just going to hang himself. Dr.
Tate and his wife, in the Irish rebellion, flying
through the woods with a sucking child, which
was just ready to expire; the mother, going to rest
it upon a rock, puts her hand upon a bottle of
warm milk, by which it was preserved. A good
woman, from whose mouth I received it, being
driven to a great extremity, all supplies failing,
was exceedingly plunged into unbelieving doubts
and fears, not seeing whence supplies could come,
when lo! at that very time, by turning some things
in a chest, unexpectedly she lights upon a piece of
gold, which supplied her present wants, till God
opened another door of supply. If these things
fall out casually, how is it they observe time so
very exactly? That is become proverbial in Scripture—" In the mount of the Lord it shall be seen,"
Gen. xxii. 14.

Eighth demand. Lastly, were these things
casual and contingent, how can it be that they
should fall out so immediately upon, and conso-
nantly to, the prayers of the saints? So that in

many providences they are able to discern a very clear answer to their prayers, and are sure they have the petitions they asked of him, 1 John v. 15.

Thus when the sea divided itself, just upon Israel's cry to heaven, Exod. xiv. 10. When so singal a victory is given to Asa, immediately upon that pathetical cry to heaven, "Help us, O Lord, our God!" 2 Chron. xiv. 11, 12. When Ahithophel shall go and hang himself just upon that prayer of distressed David, 2 Sam. xv. 31. When Haman shall fall, and his plot be broken, just upon the fast kept by Mordecai and Esther, Esth. iv. 16. Our own Speed, in his History of Britain, tells us that Richard I. besieged a castle with his army; they offered to surrender, if he would save their lives; he refuses, and threatens to hang them all. Upon this, an archer charged his bow with a square arrow, making first his prayer to God, that he would direct the shot, and deliver the innocent from oppression: it struck the king himself, whereof he died, and they were delivered. Abraham's servant prayed for success, and see how it was answered, Gen. xxiv. 45. Peter was cast into prison, and prayer was made for him by the church, and see the event, Acts xii. 5–12. I could easily add to these the wonderful examples of the return of prayers which was observed in Luther, and Dr. Winter, in Ireland, and many more; but I judge it needless, because most Christians have a stock of experience of their own, and are well assured that many of the providences that befall them are, and can be, no other than the return of their prayers.

And now, who can be dissatisfied on this point, that wisely considers these things? Must we not

conclude that, " he withdraweth not his eye from
the righteous?" Job xxxvi. 7, and that "the eyes
of the Lord run to and fro throughout the whole
earth to show himself strong in the behalf of them
whose heart is perfect towards him," 2 Chron. xvi.
9. His providences proclaim him to be a God
hearing prayers.

THE SECOND GENERAL HEAD.

Having proved that the concerns of the saints,
in this world, are certainly conducted by the wisdom and care of a special Providence, my next
work is to show you in what affairs and concerns
of theirs the providence of God doth more especially appear, or what are the most remarkable
performances of Providence for them in this
world.

And here I am not led directly by my text to
speak of the most internal and spiritual performances of Providence, immediately relating to the
souls of his people, though they all relate to their
souls mediately and eventually, but of the more
visible and external performances of Providence
for them.   And it is not to be supposed that I
should touch all these neither; they are more than
the sands: but that which I aim at, is to discourse
to you some more special and more observable
performances of Providence for you. And we
shall begin with

I. THE FIRST PERFORMANCE OF PROVIDENCE.

Let us consider how well Providence hath performed the first work that ever it did for us, in our
formation and protection in the womb.   Certainly
this is a very glorious and admirable performance

it is what the psalmist admires: "My substance was not hid from thee when I was made in secret, and curiously wrought in the lowest parts of the earth." Psal. cxxxix. 15. The womb is so called upon this account, because as curious artists, when they have some choice piece in hand, perfect it in private, and then bring it into the light for all to gaze at, so it was here. And there are two things admirable in this performance of Providence for us.

1. The rare structure and excellent composition of the body: " I am wonderfully made." The word in the Hebrew is very full. The Vulgate renders it, painted as with a needle, that is, richly embroidered with nerves and veins. Oh! the curious workmanship that is in that one part, the eye! How has it forced some to acknowledge a God, upon the examination of it! Providence, when it went about this work, had its model or pattern before it, according to which it moulded every part, as it is in ver. 16. " In thy book were all my members written." Hast thou an integral perfection and fulness of members? It is because God wrote them all in his book, or limned out thy body, according to that exact model, which he drew of thee in his own gracious purpose, before thou hadst a being. Had an eye, an ear, a hand, or a foot, been wanting in the platform, thou hadst now been sadly sensible of the defect; this world had been but a dungeon to thee without those windows; thou hadst lived, as many do, an object of pity to others, If thou hast low thoughts of this mercy, ask the blind, the deaf, the lame, and the dumb, the value and worth of those mercies, and they will tell thee. There is a world of cost be-

stowed upon thy very body. Thou mightest
have been cast into another mould, and created a
worm or a toad. I remember Luther tells us of
two cardinals, riding in great pomp to the Council
of Constance, and, by the way, they heard a man
in the fields bitterly weeping and wailing. When
they came to him, they found him intently viewing an ugly toad! and asking why he wept so
bitterly, he told them, his heart was melted with
this consideration, that God had not made him
such a loathsome and deformed creature. This is
what I love to weep at, said he : whereupon, one
of them cries out, Well said the father, The un-
learned will rise and take heaven, and we, with
all our learning, shall be cast into hell. No part
of the common lump was so figured and polished
as man is. Galen gave Epicurus a hundred years'
time to imagine a more commodious situation,
configuration, or composition, of any one member
of a human body ; and if all the angels had studied
to this day, they could not have cast the body of
man into a more curious mould.

2. And yet all this is but the enameling of the
case, or polishing the casket wherein the rare
jewel lies. Providence hath not only built the
house, but brought the inhabitant (I mean the
soul) into the possession of it. A glorious piece
it is, that bears the very image of God upon it,
being all in all, and all in every part. How noble
are its faculties and affections! How nimble, various, and indefatigable are its motions ! How com-
prehensive is its capacity ! It is a companion for
angels, nay, capable of espousals to Christ, and
eternal communion with God. It is the wonder of
earth, and the envy of hell.

Suppose now (and why should you not suppose

what you so frequently behold in the world?) that
Providence had so permitted and ordered it, that
thy soul had entered into thy body with one or
two of its faculties wounded and defective? Suppose its understanding had been cracked; what a
miserable life hadst thou lived in this world, neither capable of service nor comfort. And truly,
when I have considered those works of Providence, in bringing into the world, in all countries
and ages, some such spectacles of pity; some deprived of the use of reason, and differing from
beasts in little more than shape and figure; and
others, though sound in their understandings, yet
deformed or defective in their bodies, monstrous,
misshapen, and loathsome creatures; I can resolve the design of this providence into nothing
beside a demonstration of his sovereign power,
except they be designed as foils to set off the
beauty of other rare and exquisite pieces, and intended to stand before your eyes as monitors of
God's mercy to you, that your hearts, as often as
you beheld them, might be melted into thankfulness for so distinguishing favour to you.

Look then, but not proudly, upon thine outside
and inside; see and admire what Providence hath
done for thee, and how well it hath performed the
first service that ever it did for thee in this world!
And yet this was not all it did for thee before thou
sawest this world: it preserved thee as well as
formed thee in the womb, else thou hadst been as
those embryos Job speaks of, that never saw the
light, Job iii. 16. Abortives go for nothing in the
world, and there are multitudes of them; some
that never had a reasonable soul breathed into
them, but only the rudiments and rough draught of
the body; these come not into the account of men,

but perish as the beast doth. Others that die in, or shortly after they come out of the womb, and though their life was but for a moment, yet that moment entails an eternity upon them. And had this been your case, as it is the case of millions, then, supposing your salvation, yet had you been utterly unserviceable to God in the world ; none had been the better for you, nor you the better for any in the world ; you had been utterly incapable for all that good which, throughout your life, you have either done to others, or received from others.

And if we consider the nature of that obscure life we lived in the womb, how small an accident, had it been permitted by Providence, had extinguished our life, like a bird in the shell ! We cannot therefore but admire the tender care of Providence over us, and say with the Psalmist, "Thou hast covered me in my mother's womb," Psal. cxxxix. 13, and not only so, but, "Thou art he that took me out of my mother's womb," Psal. xxii. 9. He preserved thee there to the fulness of time, and, when that time was come, brought thee safely through manifold hazards into that place in the world which he from eternity espied for thee ; which leads us to the second performance.

II. The next great performance of Providence for the people of God, respects the place and time in which it ordered their nativity to fall. And truly this is no small concern to every one of us, but of vast consequence, either to our good or evil, though it be of little minded by most men. I am persuaded the thoughts of few Christians penetrate deep enough into this providence, but slide too slightly and superficially over an abyss of much mercy,

4

rich and manifold mercy, wrapped up in this gracious performance of Providence for them.

Ah friends ! can you think it an indifferent thing
into what part of the world you are cast ? Is there
no odds upon what spot of the creation, or what
age of the world your lot had fallen ? It may be
you have not seriously bethought yourselves about
this matter. And because this point is so seldom
touched, I will therefore dive a little more particularly and distinctly into it, and endeavour to warm
your affections with a representation of the many
and rich benefits you owe to this one performance
of Providence for you.

And we will consider it under a double respect
or relation ; as it respects your present comfort in
this world, and as it relates to your eternal happiness in the world to come.

1. This performance of Providence for you doth
very much concern your present comfort in this
world. All the rooms in this great house are not
alike pleasant and commodious for the inhabitants
of it. You read of "the dark places of the earth,
which are full of the habitations of cruelty," Psal.
lxxiv. 20, and many such dismal places are found
in the habitable earth. What a vast tract of the
world lies as a waste wilderness !

Suppose your mothers had brought you forth in
America among the savage Indians, who herd together as brute beasts ; are scorched with heat and
starved with cold, being naked, destitute, and defenceless. How poor, miserable, and unprovided
of earthly comforts and accommodations are many
millions of the inhabitants of this world ! What
mercies do you enjoy in respect of the amenity,
fertility, temperature, and civility of the place of

your habitation? What is it but a garden enclosed out of a wilderness? I may, without partiality or vanity, say, God hath, even upon temporal accounts, provided you with one of the most healthful, pleasant, and, in all respects, the best furnished room in all the great house of this world.

You are here provided with necessary and comfortable accommodations for your bodies, that a great part of the world are unacquainted with. It is not with the poorest among us, as it is said to be with the poor in a foreign land, whose poverty pinches and bites with such sharp teeth, that their poor cry at their doors, Give me, and cut me! give me, and kill me!

Say not, the barbarous nations in this excel you; that they possess the mines of silver and gold, which, it may be, you think enough to compensate for all other inconveniences of life. Alas, poor creatures! better had it been for them if their country had brought forth briers and thorns, instead of gold, silver, and precious stones; for this hath been the occasion of ruining all their other comforts in this world. This hath invited their cruel, avaricious enemies among them, under whose servitude they groan and die without mercy; and thousands of them have chosen death rather than life, on the terms they enjoyed it. And why might not your lot have fallen there, as well as where it is? Are not they made of the same clay, and endowed with as good a nature as yourselves? Oh what a distinction hath Divine Mercy made, where nature made none! Consider, ungrateful man, thou mightest have fallen into some of those regions where a tainted air frequently cloys the jaws of death, where the inhabitants differ very little from the beasts in the manner of their living.

but God hath provided for thee, and given the poorest among us far better accommodations of life than the greatest among them are ordinarily provided with. Oh, what hath Providence done for you!

But all that I have said is very inconsiderable in comparison with the spiritual mercies and advantages you here enjoy for your souls. Oh! this is such an advantageous cast of Providence for you, as obliges you to a thankful acknowledgment of it to all eternity! For, let us here make but a few suppositions, in the case before us, and the glory of Providence will shine like a sunbeam full in your faces.

(1.) Suppose it had been your lot to have fallen into any of those vast continents, possessed by pagans and heathens at this day, who bow down to the stock of a tree, and worship the host of heaven. This is the case of many millions; for pagan idolaters (as that searching scholar Mr. Berewood informs us, in his Inquiries) do not only fill the circumference of nine hundred miles in Europe, but almost the one half of Africa, more than the half of Asia, and almost the whole of America.*

Oh! how deplorable had thy case been, if a pagan idolatress had brought thee forth, and idolatry had been sucked in with thy mother's milk! Then, in all probability, thou hadst been at this day worshipping devils, and posting with full speed in the direct road to damnation. For these are the people of God's wrath: "Pour out thy fury upon the heathen that know thee not, and upon the families that call not upon thy name," Jer. x. 25. How ·

* America is much improved since Mr. Flavel's time.—*Editor.*

dreadful is that imprecation against them, which takes hold of them, and all that is theirs! "Confounded be all they that serve graven images, that boast themselves of idols," Psal. xcvii. 7.

(2.) Or suppose your lot had fallen among Mahometans who, next to pagans, spread over the greatest tract of the earth; for though Arabia bred that unclean bird, yet it was not that cage that could long contain him; for not only the Arabians, but the Persians, Turks, and Tartars, do all bow down their backs under that grand impostor. This poison hath dispersed itself through the veins of Asia, over a great part of Africa, even the circumference of seven thousand miles, and stops not there, but hath tainted a considerable part of Europe also.

Had your lot fallen here, oh what unhappy men and women had you been, notwithstanding the natural amenity and pleasantness of your native soil! You had then adored a grand impostor, and died in a fool's paradise. Instead of God's lively oracles, you had been, as they now are, deceived to your eternal ruin with such fond, mad, and wild dreams, as whosoever considers, would think the authors had more need of manacles and fetters, than arguments or sober answers.

(3.) Or if neither of these had been your lot, but you had been placed in a country which is christianized by profession, but nevertheless for the most part overrun by popish idolatry and antichristian delusions; what unhappy men and women had you been, had you sucked a popish breast! For this people are to be the subjects of the vials of God's wrath, to be poured out successively upon them, as you may read Rev. xvi. and the Scriptures, in round and plain language, tell us what their fate must be: "And for this cause God

4*

shall send them strong delusion, that they shall believe a lie, that they all might be damned who believed not the truth, but had pleasure in unrighteousness," 2 Thess. ii. 11, 12.

Nay, you might have fallen into the same land in which your habitation now is, and yet have had no advantage by it as to salvation, if he who chose the bounds of your habitations had not also graciously determined the times for you, Acts xvii. 26. For,

(4.) Suppose your lot had fallen where it is, during the pagan state of England, whose inhabitants for many hundred years were gross and vile idolators. Thick darkness overspread the people of this island, and, as in other countries, the devil was worshipped, and his lying oracles zealously attended upon.

The shaking of the top of Jupiter's oak in Dodona; the caldron smitten with the rod in the hand of Jupiter's image; the laurel and fountain in Daphne; these were the ordinances on which the poor deluded wretches waited. So in this nation they worshipped idols also; the sun and moon were adored for gods, with many other abominable idols, which our ancestors worshipped, and whose memorials are not to this day quite obliterated among us.

(5.) Or suppose our lot had fallen in those later miserable days, in which Queen Mary sent so many hundreds to heaven in a fiery chariot, and the poor Protestants skulked up and down in holes and woods to preserve them from popish inquisitors, who, like blood-hounds, hunted up and down through all the cities, towns, and villages of the nation to seek out the poor sheep of Christ for a prey.

But such hath been the special care of Provi-

dence towards us, that our turn to be brought upon
the stage of this world was graciously reserved for
better days: so that if we had had our own option
we could not have chosen for ourselves as Providence hath.   We are not only furnished with the
best room in this great house, but, before we were
put into it, it was swept with the besom of national
reformation from idolatry ; yea, and washed by the
blood of martyrs from popish filthiness, and adorn-
ed with gospel lights, shining in as great lustre in
our days, as ever they did since the apostles' days.
You might have been born in England for many
ages, and not have found a Christian in it: yea and
since Christianity was here owned, and not have
met a Protestant in it.   Oh what an obligation hath
Providence laid you under by such a merciful performance as this for you !

If you say, All this indeed is true, but what is
this to eternal salvation ? do not multitudes that enjoy these privileges eternally perish notwithstanding them ? yea, and perish with an aggravation of
sin and misery beyond other sinners?

True, they do so; and it is of very sad consideration that it should be so; but yet we cannot
deny this to be a very choice and singular mercy,
to be born in such a land, and at such a time ; for,
let us consider what helps for salvation men here
enjoy beyond what they could enjoy had their
lot fallen according to the fore-mentioned suppositions.

[1.] Here we enjoy the ordinary means of salvation, which elsewhere men are denied and cut
off from ; so that if any among the heathens be
saved and brought to Christ, it must be in some
miraculous or extraordinary way ; for, " How

shall they believe in him of whom they have not
heard? and how shall they hear without a preacher?" Rom. x. 14. Alas! were there a desire
awakened in any of their hearts, after a gospel-
discovery of salvation, (which ordinarily is not,
nor can be rationally supposed,) yet, poor creatures! they might travel from sea to sea to hear
the word, and not find it: whereas you can hardly
miss the opportunities of hearing the gospel; sermons meet you frequently, so that you can scarcely shun or avoid the ordinances and instruments
of your salvation. And is this nothing? Christ
even forces himself upon us.

[2.] Here, in this age of the world, the common
prejudices against Christianity are removed by the
advantage it hath of a public profession among the
people, and protection by the laws of the country;
whereas were your habitation among Jews, Mahometans, or heathen idolators, you would find
Christ and Christianity the common odium of the
country, every one defying and deriding both name
and thing; and such yourselves likely had been,
if your birth and education had been among them;
for you may observe, that whatever is traditionally
delivered down from father to son, every one is
fond of, and zealous in its defence. The Jews,
Heathens, and Mahometans, are at this day so te-
nacious of their errors, that with spitting, hissing,
and clapping of hands, and all other signs of in-
dignation and abhorrence, they chase away all
others from among them.

Is it not then a special mercy to you, to be cast
into such a country and age, where, as a learned
divine observes, the true religion hath the same
advantages over every false one, as in other coun-

tries they have over it? Here you have the presence of precious means, and the absence of soul-
destroying prejudices—two singular mercies.

[3.] Here, in this age of the world, Christianity
bespeaks you as soon as you are capable of any
sense, or impressions, of religion upon you, and
so by a happy anticipation blocks up the passages
by which a false religion would certainly enter.
Here you suck in the first notions and principles
of Christianity, even with the mother's milk. And
certainly such a prepossession is a choice advantage. "Train up a child in the way he should
go, and when he is old he will not depart from it,"
Prov. xxii. 6.

[4.] Here you have, or may have, the help and
assistance of Christians to direct your way, resolve
your doubts, support your burdens, and help you
through those difficulties that attend the new birth.
Alas! if a poor soul had any beginnings, or faint
workings and stirrings after Christ and true religion, in many other countries, the hand of every
man would presently be against him, and none
would be found to relieve, assist, or encourage, as
you may see in that example of Galeacius. The
nearest relations would, in that case, prove the
greatest enemies, the country would quickly hoot
at him as a monster, and cry, Away with the here-
tic to the prison or stake.

Whether these eventually prove blessings to
your souls or not, certain I am, that, in themselves, they are singular mercies, and helps to salvation, though denied to millions around you. So
that, if Plato, when he was near his death, could
bless God for three things, namely, That he was
a man, and not a beast; that he was born in
Greece; and that he was brought up in the time

of Socrates: much more cause have you to admire Providence that you are men, and not beasts;
that you were born here; and brought up in
gospel days here. This is a land the Lord hath
espied for you, as the expression is, Ezek. xx. 6,
and concerning it, you have abundant cause to
say, as in another case the Psalmist doth, "the
lines are fallen to me in pleasant places, and I
have a goodly heritage," Psal. xvi. 6.

III. The next observable performance of Providence, which must be heedfully adverted to, and
weighed, is the designation of the stock and family
out of which we should spring and rise. And truly
this is of special consideration, both as to our temporal and eternal good; for whether the families in
which we grew up were great or small in Israel;
whether our parents were of higher or lower class
and rank among men, yet if they were such as
feared God, and wrought righteousness, if they
took any care to educate you righteously, and
trained you up "in the nurture and admonition of
the Lord," you are bound to reckon it among your
chief mercies, that you descended from such parents, for from this spring a double stream of mercy
rises to you. Temporal and external mercies to
your outward man. You cannot but know, that as
godliness entails a blessing, so wickedness and unrighteousness, a curse, upon posterity; an instance
of the former you have in Gen. xvii. 18, 20. On
the contrary, you have the threatening, Zech. v. 4,
and both together in this passage: "The curse of
the Lord is in the house of the wicked, but he blesseth the habitation of the just," Prov. iii. 33. True
it is, that both these imply the children's treading
in the steps of their parents, according to Ezekiel
xviii, but how frequently is it seen, that wicked

men bring up their children vainly and wickedly;
so that, as it is said of Abijam, " He walked in all
the sins of his father, which he had done before
him," 1 Kings xv. 3, and so the curse is entailed
from generation to generation.   To escape this
curse is a choice providence.

But especially take notice, what a stream of
spiritual blessings and mercies flows from this
providence to the inner man.   O! it is no common
mercy to descend from pious parents! some of us
do not only owe our natural life to them, as instruments of our being, but our spiritual and eternal
life also.   It was no small mercy to Timothy that
he descended from such progenitors, 2 Tim. i. 5,
nor to Augustine that he had such a mother as
Monica, who planted in his mind the precepts of
life with her words, watered them with her tears,
and nourished them with her example.   We will
a little more particularly inspect this mercy, and,
in so doing, we shall find manifold mercies contained in it.

1. What a mercy was it to us to have parents,
who prayed for us before they had us, as well as
in our infancy, when we could not pray for ourselves!   Thus did Abraham, Gen. xv. 2, and Han-
nah, 1 Sam. i. 10, 11, and some here, likely, are
the fruits and returns of their parents' prayers.
This was that holy course they continued all their
days for you, carrying all your concerns, especially your eternal ones, before the Lord with their
own, and pouring out their souls to God so affectionately for you, when their eye-strings and heart-
strings were breaking.   O! put a value upon
such mercies, for they are precious!   It is a greater
mercy to descend from praying parents, than from
nobles.   See Job's pious practice, Job i. 5.

2. What a special mercy was it to us to have the excrescences of corruption nipped in the bud, by their pious and careful discipline! We now understand what a critical and dangerous season youth is, the wonderful proneness of that age to every thing that is evil. Why else are they called youthful lusts? 2 Tim. ii. 22. When David asks, " Wherewith shall a young man cleanse his way?" it is plainly enough implied in the very question, that the way he takes lies through the pollutions of the world in his youth, Psal. cxix. 9. When you find a David praying, that God would "not remember the sins of his youth," Psal. xxv. 7, and a Job bitterly complaining, that God " made him to possess the sins of his youth," Job xiii. 26, sure you cannot but reflect, with a very thankful heart, upon those happy means by which the corruption of your nature was happily prevented, or restrained, in your youth.

3. And how great a mercy was it, that we had parents who carefully instilled the good knowledge of God into our souls, in our tender years! How careful was Abraham of this duty! Gen. xviii. 19. And David, 1 Chron. xxviii. 9. We have some of us had parents, who might say to us, as the apostle, " My little children, of whom I travail again in birth, till Christ be formed in you," Gal. iv. 19. As they longed for us before they had us, and rejoiced in us, when they had us, so they could not endure to think that, when they could have us no more, the devil should. As they thought no pains, care, or cost, too much for our bodies to feed them, clothe, and heal them ; so did they think no prayers, counsels, or tears, too much for our souls, that they might be saved. They knew a parting time would come between them

and us, and did strive to make it as easy and comfortable to them as they could, by leaving us in
Christ, and within the blessed bond of his covenant.   They were not glad that we had health, and
indifferent whether we had grace.   They as sensibly felt the miseries of our souls as of our bodies ;
and nothing was more desirable to them than that
they might say in the great day, Lord, here am I,
and the children which thou hast given me.

4. And was it not a special favour to us to have
parents, that went before us as a pattern of holiness, and beat the path to heaven for us by their
examples ; who could say to us, " What things
ye have heard and seen in me, do," Phil. iv. 9,
and " Be ye followers of us, as we are of Christ,"
1 Cor. xi. 1.   The parent's life is the child's copy.
O ! it is no common mercy to have a fair copy set
before us, especially in the moulding age !   We
saw what they did, as well as heard what they
said.   It was Abraham's commendation that " he
commanded his children, and his household after
him, to keep the way of the Lord ;" and such
mercies some of us have had also.

Ah ! my friends, let me beg you that you will
set special remarks upon this providence, which is
so graciously wrought for you ; and, that your
hearts may be more thoroughly warmed in the
sense of it, compare your condition with others,
and seriously bethink yourselves,

(1.) How many children there are among us
who are drawn headlong to hell by their cruel and
ungodly parents, who teach them to curse and
swear as soon as they can speak !   Many families
there are, wherein little other language is heard
but what is the dialect of hell.   These, like the
old logs and small twigs, are preparing for the fire

5

of hell, where they must burn together. Of such children, that Scripture will one day be verified, Except they repent, "they shall go to the generation of their fathers, where they shall not see light," Psal. xlix. 19.

(2.) And how many families are there, though not so profane, who yet breed up their children vainly and sensually, as in Job xxi. 11, &c. and take no care what becomes of their souls, so they can but provide for their bodies! If they can but teach them to carry their bodies, no matter if the devil direct their souls; if they can but leave them lands or moneys, they think they have very fully discharged their duties. O! what will the language be wherewith such parents and children shall greet each other, at the judgment-seat, and in hell, for ever!

(3.) And how many are there, who are more sober, and yet hate the least appearances of godliness in their children! who, instead of cherishing, do all they can to break bruised reeds, to quench smoking flax, to stifle and strangle the first appearances and offers they make towards Christ! who had rather accompany them to their graves, than to Christ, doing all that in them lies, Herod-like, to kill Christ in the cradle! Ah, sirs! you little know what a mercy you do, or have enjoyed, in godly parents, and what a good lot Providence cast for you in this concern of your bodies and souls!

If any shall say, this is not their case, they had little help heavenward from their parents; to such I shall thus reply: If you had little furtherance, yet own it as a special providence, that you had no hindrance; or, if you had opposition, yet admire the grace of God in plucking you out by a wonderful distinguishing hand of mercy from among them, and keeping alive the languishing sparks of grace amidst the floods of opposition; and learn from hence, if God give you a posterity of your own, to be so much the more strict and careful of relative duties, by how much you have sensibly felt the want of it in yourselves.

But seeing such a train of blessings, both as to this life and that to come, follows upon a holy education of children, I will not dismiss the point, till I have discharged my duty, in exhorting parents and children to their duties.

EXHORTATION TO PARENTS.

And, first, for you that are parents, or to whom the education of children is committed, I beseech you to reflect what an important duty lies on you; and, that I may effectually impress it, consider,

1. How near the relation is between you and your children, and, therefore, how much you are concerned in their happiness or misery. Consider but the Scripture account of the dearness of such relations, expressed by longings for them, as it is in Gen. xv. 2, and Gen. xxx. 1, and by our joy when we have them, as Christ expresses it, John xvi. 21, the high value set on them, Gen. xlii. 38, the sympathy with them in all their troubles, Mark ix. 22, and by our sorrow at parting. Gen. xxxvii. 35. Now shall all this be to no purpose? For to what purpose do we desire them before we have them; rejoice in them when we have them; value them so highly; sympathize with them so tenderly; grieve for their death so excessively, if, in the mean time, no care be taken what shall become of them to eternity?

2. How God hath charged you with their souls, as well as bodies; and this appears by precepts directly laid upon you, Deut. vi. 6, 7, and Eph. vi. 4, and by precepts laid on them to obey you, Eph. vi. 1, which plainly imply your duty, as well as express theirs.

3. What shall comfort you at the parting time, if they die, through your neglect, in a Christless condition? Oh! this is the cutting consideration, My child is in hell, and I did nothing to prevent it; I helped him thither! Duly discharged is the only root of comfort in that day.

4. If you neglect to instruct them in the way of holiness, will the devil neglect to instruct them in the way of wickedness? No. If you will not teach them to pray, he will to curse, swear, and lie. If ground be uncultivated, weeds will spring.

5. If the season of their youth be neglected, how little probability is there of any good fruit afterwards! That is the moulding age, Prov. xxii. 6. How few are converted in old age! A twig is brought to any form, but grown trees will not bow.

6. You are instrumental causes of all their spiritual misery, and that by generation and imitation: they lie spiritually dead of the plague, which you brought home among them: "Behold, I was shapen in iniquity, and in sin did my mother conceive me," Psal. li. 5.

7. There is none in the world so likely, as you, to be instruments of their eternal good. You have peculiar advantages that no others have, as the interest you have in their affections: your opportunities to instil the knowledge of Christ into them, being daily with them, Deut. vi. 7, and

your knowledge of their tempers.   If therefore you
neglect, who shall help them?

8. The consideration of the great day should
move your feelings of pity for them.   O remember that text, "I saw the dead, small and great,
stand before God," Rev. xx. 12, &c.   What a sad
thing will it be to see your dear children at Christ's
left hand!   O friends, do your utmost to prevent
this misery!   "Knowing the terrors of the Lord,
we persuade men," 2 Cor. v. 11.

EXHORTATION TO CHILDREN.

And you, children especially you that sprang
from religious parents, I beseech you to obey their
counsels, and tread in the steps of their pious examples.   To press this, I offer these considerations:

1. Your disobedience to them is a resisting of
God's authority.   "Children, obey your parents
in the Lord," Ephes. vi. 1, there is the command; your rebellion, therefore, runs higher than
you think.   It is not man, but God, that you
disobey; and for your disobedience God will
punish you.   It may be, their tenderness will not
suffer them, or you are grown beyond their cor-
rection; all they can do is to complain to God;
and, if so, he will handle you more severely than
they could do.

2. Your sin is greater than the sin of young
heathens and infidels, and so will your account be
also.   O better (if a wicked child) that thou hadst
been the offspring of savage Indians, nay, of
beasts, than of such parents.   So many counsels
disobeyed, hopes and prayers frustrated, will turn
to sad aggravations.

3. It is usual with God to retaliate men's dis-

obedience to their parents in kind; commonly our own children shall pay us home for it. I have read in a grave author, of a wicked wretch that dragged his father along the house: the father begged him not to draw him beyond such a place, for, said he, I dragged my father no further. Oh! the sad, but just retributions of God!

And, for you, in whose hearts grace hath been planted by the blessing of education, I beseech you to admire God's goodness to you in this providence. Oh! what a happy lot has God cast for you! How few children are partakers of your mercies!

See that you honour such parents; the tie is double upon you so to do. Be you the joy of their hearts, and comfort of their lives, if living; if not, yet still remember the mercy while you live, and tread in their pious paths, that you and they may both rejoice together in the great day, and bless God for each other to all eternity.

IV. The next remarkable performance of Providence for the people of God, which I will instance, shall be with respect to its ordering the occasions, instruments, and means of their conversion.

In nothing doth Providence shine forth more gloriously in this world, than it doth in this performance for the people of God. How curiously soever its hand had moulded your bodies, how tenderly soever it had preserved them, and how bountifully soever it had provided for them; if it had not also ordered some means or other for your conversion, all the former favours and benefits it had done for you had signified little. This, oh this, is the most excellent benefit you ever received from its hand! You are more beholden to

it for this, than for all your other mercies. And,
in opening this performance of Providence, I cannot but think your hearts must be deeply affected.
This is a subject, which every gracious heart loves
to steep its thoughts in. It is certainly the sweetest
history that ever they repeated ; they love to think
and talk of it. The places where, and instruments
by whom this work was wrought, are exceedingly
endeared to them for the work's sake ; yea, endeared to that degree, that, for many years after,
their hearts have melted, when they have but
passed occasionally by those places, or but seen
the faces of those persons, who were used as instruments, in the hand of Providence, for their
good. As no doubt but Jacob's Bethel was ever
after that night sweet to his thoughts, so other
saints have had their Bethels as well as he. Oh
blessed places, times, and instruments ! Oh the
deep, the sweet impressions, never to be razed
out of the memory or heart, that this providence
has made upon those on whom it wrought this
blessed effect at years of discrection, and in a more
sensible way !

But lest any poor soul should be discouraged
under the display of this providence, because he
cannot remember the time, place, instruments, and
manner wherein, and by which conversion-work
was wrought, I will therefore premise this necessary distinction, to prevent injury to some, whilst
I design benefit to others. Conversion, as to the
subject of it, may be considered two ways ; either
as it is more sensibly wrought in persons of riper
years, who, in their youthful days, were more
profane and vile ; or upon persons in their tender
years, into whose hearts grace was more insen-
sibly and indiscernibly instilled by God's blessing

upon pious education. In the former sort, the distinct acts of the Spirit, as illuminating, convincing, humbling, drawing them to Christ, and sealing them, are more evident and discernible; in the latter, more obscure and confused. They can remember that God gave them an esteem and liking of godly persons, care of duty, and conscience of sin; but as to the time, place, instruments, and manner of the work, they can give but a slender account of them. However, if the work be savingly wrought in them, there is no reason they should be troubled because the circumstances of it are not so evident to them as they are to others. Let the substance and reality of the work appear, and there is no reason to afflict yourselves, because the evidence of such circumstances is wanting.

But, yet, when the circumstances as well as substance are clear to men; when we can call to remembrance the time when, the place where, the instrument by whom that work was wrought, it must needs be exceedingly sweet; and they cannot but yield a fresh delight to the soul, every time they are reflected upon.

There are many of the following occasions which, it may be, we took for stragglers, when they first befell us; but they proved scouts sent out from the main body of providence, which they make way for.

Now there are divers things in those providences, that are connected with this work, which are exceedingly sweet and taking; as,

1. The wonderful strangeness and unaccountableness of this work of Providence in casting us into the way, and ordering the occasions, yea, the minutest circumstances about this work. This

you find in Acts viii. 26—30, &c. The eunuch,
at that very instant when he was reading the prophet Isaiah, hath an interpreter, one among a thousand, that joins his chariot just as his mind was,
by a fit occasion, prepared to receive the first light
of the knowledge of Christ.

And how strange was that change, how far soever it went, upon Naaman the Syrian, recorded
2 Kings v. 1—4, that the Syrians, in their incur-
sions, should bring away this girl, (likely her
beauty was the inducement,) and she must be presented to Naaman's wife, and relate to her the
power of God, that accompanied the prophet;
though you find in that particular case there had
never been an instance given before, Luke iv. 27.
Doubtless the whole of this affair was guided by
the signal direction of Providence.

So for the conversion of the Samaritans it is observed, John iv. 4, Christ must needs go that way,
because it lay just in the road between Judea and
Galilee, and that at the sixth hour, that is, high
noon, he rests himself upon Jacob's well, still
seeming to have no other design but his own refreshment, by sitting and drinking there; but, O!
what a train of blessed providences follows this,
which seemed but an accidental thing! First, the
woman of Samaria, and then, many more in that
city, are brought to believe in Christ, as you find
in ver. 29 and 41.

It is noted by Melchior Adam, in the life of
Junius, how very an atheist he grew in his younger
years; but, in order to his conversion to God, first
a wonderful preservation of his life, in a public
tumult at Lyons, in France, must make way, which
forces from him the acknowledgment of a Deity;

then his father sends for him home, and with much
gentleness persuades him to read the Scriptures;
he lights upon the first of John, and with it, he
sensibly feels a divine, supernatural majesty and
power seizing his soul, which brought him over
by a complete conversion to Jesus Christ. Thus,
as the woman of Tekoa told David, "doth God
devise means to bring back his banished."

Lavater tells us, that many Spanish soldiers,
going into the wars of Germany, were there converted to Christ, by falling into the cities and towns
inhabited by godly ministers and Christians.

Mr. Robert Bolton, though an excellent scholar,
yet in his younger years was a very irreligious
person, and a jeerer of holy men; but, being cast
into the company of the godly Mr. Peacock, was,
by him, brought to repentance, and proved a
famous instrument in the church of Christ.

A scrap of paper accidentally coming to view
hath been used as an occasion of conversion. This
was the case of a minister in Wales, who had two
livings, but took little care of either. He being at
a fair, bought something at a pedlar's standing, and
rent off a leaf of Mr. Perkins's catechism to wrap
it in, and reading a line or two in it, God set it
home so as it did the work.

The marriage of a godly man, into a carnal
family, hath been ordered by Providence for the
conversion and salvation of many therein. Thus we
read, in the life of that renowned English worthy,
Mr. John Bruen, that, in his second match, it was
agreed that he should have one year's diet in his
mother-in-law's house. During his abode there that
year, (saith Mr. Clark,) the Lord was pleased, by
his means, graciously to work upon her soul, as

also upon his wife's sister, and half sister, their brothers, Mr. William and Mr. Thomas Fox, with one or two of the servants in that family.

The reading of a good book hath been the means of bringing others to Christ. And thus we find many of the German divines converted by reading Luther's books. Yea, and what is more strange, Mr. Sleyden, in his Commentary, tells us, that Vergerius, though he were present an eye and ear witness to that doleful case of Spira, which one would think should move a stone, yet still continued so firm to the Pope's interest, that when he fell into some suspicion among the cardinals, he resolved to purge himself by writing a book against the German apostates ; but, whilst he read the protestant books, out of no other design but to confute them, whilst he is weighing the arguments, he is himself convinced and brought to Christ. He, finding himself thus overcome by the truth, imparts his conviction to his brother, a zealous papist also; this brother deplores the misery of his case, and seeks to reclaim him ; but Vergerius entreating him to weigh well the protestant arguments, he also yields ; and so both immediately betook themselves to preach justification, by the free grace of God, through the blood of Christ.

Yea, not only the reading of a book, or hearing of a minister, but, which is most remarkable, the very mistake or forgetfulness of a minister hath been improved by providence for this end and purpose. Augustine, once preaching to his congregation, forgot the argument which he first proposed, and fell upon the errors of the Manichees, beside his first intention ; by which discourse, he converted one Firmus, his auditor, who fell down at his feet weeping, and confessing he had lived a

Manichee many years. Another I knew, who, going to preach, took up another Bible than that he designed, in which, not only missing his notes, but the chapter also in which his text lay, was put to some loss thereby: but, after a short pause, he resolved to speak to any other Scripture that might be presented to him, and accordingly, read the text, " The Lord is not slack concerning his promise," 2 Pet. iii. 9, and though he had nothing prepared, yet the Lord helped him to speak both methodically and pertinently from it; by which discourse a gracious change was wrought upon one in the congregation, who hath since given good evidence of a sound conversion, and acknowledged this sermon to be the first and only means thereof.

The accompanying of others, in a neighbourly, civil visit, hath been overruled to the same end. Thus many of the Jews accompanied Mary into Bethany, designing only to manifest their civil respect, but there they met Christ, saw the things which he did, and believed on him, John xi. 45.

Mr. Firmin, in his " Real Christian," tells us of one who had lived many years in a town where Christ had been as clearly and as long preached as in any town in England. This man, when he was about seventy-six years of age, went to visit a sick neighbour. "A Christian friend of mine," saith my author, "came to see him also, and finding this old man there, whom we judged to be one that lived upon his own stock, civility, good works, &c., he purposely fell into that discourse, to show how many persons lived upon their duties, but never came to Christ. The old man, sitting by the bed-side, heard him, and God was pleased to convince him, that he was such a person, who had lived upon himself, without Christ, to that day;

and he would say afterwards, Had I died before
three-score and sixteen, I had perished, for I knew
not Christ."

The committing of a godly man to prison hath
been the method of Providence to save the soul of
a poor keeper. So Paul was made a prisoner, to
make his keeper a spiritual freeman, Acts xvi. 27.
The like success had Dr. Barnes, in Queen Mary's
days, who celebrated the Lord's Supper in prison
with his converted keeper.

The scattering of ministers and Christians, by
persecution, from cities and towns, into the ignorant and barbarous parts of the country, hath been
the way of Providence to find out and bring home
some lost sheep that were found there to Jesus
Christ, Acts viii. 1, 4. The like signal event hath
since followed upon the like scattering of godly
ministers, whereof there are many pregnant instances at this day.

A servant running away from his master, likely
upon no other design but to live an idle life, yet
falling into such places and companies as Providence ordered in a design to him unknown, hath
thereby been brought to be the servant of Christ.
This was the very case of Onesimus, who ran
away from his master Philemon, to Rome, where,
by a strange providence, (possibly a mere curiosity
to see the prisoners,) he falls into Paul's hands,
who begat him to Christ in his bonds, Philemon,
10—16.

Going to hear a sermon in *jest* hath proved
some men's conversion in *earnest*. The above-
named Mr. Firmin, in the fore-cited book, tells us
of a notorious drunkard, whom the drunkards called father, that one day would needs go to hear
what Wilson said, out of no other design, it seems,

6

but to scoff at that holy man : but, in the prayer
before sermon, his heart began to thaw, and when
he read his text, which was, " Sin no more, lest a
worse thing come unto thee," John v. 14, he
could not contain ; and in that sermon the Lord
changed his heart, though so bitter an enemy, that
the minister, on lecture days, was afraid to go to
church before his shop door.   " Lo, these are parts
of his ways, but how small a portion is known of
him !"

The dropping of some grave and weighty word,
accidentally, in the presence of vain, carnal persons ; the death of a husband, wife, or child ; a fit
of sickness, with a thousand other such like occasions, have been thus improved, by Providence,
to the conversion of souls.

And no less remarkable and wonderful are the
designs of Providence, in ordering the removes,
and governing the motions of ministers, from place
to place, in order unto the conversion of souls.
Thus, oftentimes, it carries them to places where
they intended not to go ; God having, unknown
to them, some elect vessels there, who must be
called by the gospel.

Thus Paul and Timothy, a sweet and lovely
pair, when they were travelling through Phrygia
and Galatia, were forbid to preach the word in
Asia, to which probably their minds inclined, Acts
xvi. 6, and when they essayed to go into Bithynia,
the Spirit suffered them not, ver. 7, but a man of
Macedonia, that is an angel in the shape or habit
of a man of that country, appeared to Paul in a
vision, and prayed him, saying, " Come over into
Macedonia, and help us," ver. 9, and there did
God open the heart of Lydia.

I knew a pious minister, now with God, who,

falling in his study upon a very rousing subject, intended for his own congregation, was strongly moved, when he had finished it, to go to a rude, vile, profane people, about five miles off, and first preach it to them. After many wrestlings with himself, not being willing to quench any motion that might be supposed to come from the Spirit of God, he obeyed and went to this people, who had then no minister of their own, and few durst come among them; and there did the Lord, beyond all expectation, open a door, and several profane ones received Christ in that place, and engaged this minister to a weekly lecture among them, in which many souls were won to God.

The same holy man, at another time, being upon a journey, passed by a company of vain persons, who were wrestling upon a green near the road; and just as he came near the place, one of them had thrown his antagonist, and stood triumphing in his strength and activity. This good man rode up to them, and turning his speech to this person, told him, Friend, I see you are a strong man, but let not the strong man glory in his strength: you must know, that you are not to wrestle with flesh and blood, but with principalities and powers, and spiritual wickednesses: how sad will it be, that Satan should at last trip up the heels of your hope, and give you an eternal overthrow! And, after about a quarter of an hour's serious discourse upon this subject, he left them, and went on his journey; but this discourse made such an impression, that the person had no rest till he opened his trouble to a godly minister, who, wisely following the work upon his soul, saw at last the blessed issue thereof in the gracious change of the person, whereof he afterwards gave the minister a joyful

account. Oh! how unsearchable are the methods
of Providence in this matter.

Nay, what is yet more wonderful, the providence of God hath sometimes ordered the very
malice of Satan and the wickedness of men, as an
occasion of eternal good to their souls. A very
memorable example whereof I shall here give the
reader, faithfully relating what not many years
past fell out in my own observation in this place,
to the astonishment of many spectators.

In the year 1673, there came into this port* a
ship of Poole, in her return from Virginia; in
which ship was one of that place, a lusty young
man, of twenty-three years of age, who was surgeon in the ship. This person, in the voyage, fell
into a deep melancholy, which the devil greatly
improved, to serve his own design for the ruin of
this poor man; however, it pleased the Lord to
restrain him from any attempts upon his own life,
until he arrived here. But, shortly after his arri-
val, upon the Lord's day, early in the morning,
being in bed with his brother, he took a knife prepared for that purpose, and cut his own throat,
and withal leaped out of the bed; and though the
wound was deep and large, yet thinking it might
not soon enough despatch his wretched life, des-
perately thrust it into his stomach, and so lay wal-
lowing in his own blood, till his brother awaking
made a cry for help: hereupon a physician and a
surgeon coming in, found the wound in his throat
mortal; and all they could do at present was only
to stitch it, and apply a plaster, with a design
rather to enable him to speak for a little while,
than with any expectation of cure; for, before that

* Dartmouth.

he breathed through the wound, and his voice was inarticulate.

In this condition, I found him that morning, and apprehending him to be within a few minutes of eternity, I laboured to work upon his heart the sense of his condition, telling him I had but little time to do any thing for him, and therefore desired him to let me know what his own apprehensions of his present condition were. He told me, he hoped in God for eternal life. I replied, that I feared his hopes were ungrounded, for that the Scripture tells us, " No murderer hath eternal life abiding in him," and insisting upon the aggravation and heinousness of the fact, I perceived his vain confidence began to fall, and some meltings of heart appeared in him. He then began to lament, with many tears, his sin and misery, and asked me if there might yet be hope for one that had destroyed himself, and shed his own blood. I replied, The sin indeed is great, but not unpardonable; and if the Lord gave him repentance unto life, and faith to apply to Jesus Christ, it should be certainly pardoned to him; and, finding him unacquainted with these things, I opened to him the nature and necessity of faith and repentance, which he greedily sucked in, and with great vehemency cried to God that he would work them upon his soul, and entreated me also to pray with him, and for him, that it might be so. I prayed with him, and the Lord thawed his heart exceedingly in that duty : loth he was to part with me; but the duties of the day necessitating me to leave him, I briefly summed up what was most necessary in my parting counsel to him, and took my leave, never expecting to see him more in this world.

6 *

But beyond my own, and all men's expectations, he continued all that day, and panted most ardently after Jesus Christ; no discourses pleased him but Christ and faith; and in this frame I found him in the evening. He rejoiced greatly to see me again, and entreated me to continue my discourses upon these subjects; and, after all, he told me, Sir, the Lord hath given me repentance for this sin; yea, and for every other sin. I see the evil of sin now, so as I never saw it before. Oh! I loathe myself; I am a vile creature in my own eyes; I do also believe; Lord, help my unbelief. I am heartily willing to take Christ upon his own terms. One thing only troubles me. I doubt this bloody sin will not be pardoned. Will Jesus Christ, saith he, apply his blood to me, that have shed my own blood? I told him, Christ shed his blood even for them that with wicked hands had shed the blood of Christ; and that was a sin of deeper guilt than his. Well, saith he, I will cast myself upon Christ; let him do by me what he will. And so I parted with him that night.

Next morning, the wounds were to be opened; and then the opinion of the surgeons was, he would immediately expire.

Accordingly, at his desire, I came that morning, and found him in a most serious frame. I prayed with him, and then the wound in his stomach was opened, but, by this time, the ventricle itself was swollen out of the orifice of the wound, and lay like a livid, discoloured mass upon the body, and was also cut through; so that all concluded it was impossible for him to live; however, they stitched the wound in the stomach, enlarged the orifice, and fomented it, and wrought it again into his body, and so stitching up the skin, left him to the disposal of Providence.

But so it was, that both the deep wound in his throat, and this in his stomach, healed; and the more dangerous wound sin had made upon his soul, was, I trust, effectually healed also. I spent many hours with him in that sickness; and, after his return home, received this account from Mr. Samuel Hardy, a minister in that town; part whereof I shall transcribe.

" *Dear Sir :*—I was much troubled at the sad providence in your town, but did much rejoice that he fell into such hands for his body and soul. You have taken much pains with him, and I hope, to good purpose. I think, if ever a great and thorough work was done in such a way, it is now; and if never the like, I am persuaded now it is. Never grow weary of such good works. One such instance is, methinks, enough to make you to abound in the work of the Lord all your days," &c.

Oh, how unsearchable are the ways of Providence in leading men to Christ! Let none be encouraged by this to sin, that grace may abound. These are rare and singular instances of the mercy of God, and such as no presumptuous sinner can expect to find. It is only recited here to the honour of Providence, which works for the recovery of sinners in ways that we understand not. Oh, what a reach hath Providence beyond our understandings!

2. And as Providence orders very strange occasions to awaken and rouse our souls at first, so it works no less wonderfully in carrying on the work to perfection; and this it doth two ways:

(1.) By quickening and reviving dying convictions and troubles for sin. Souls, after their first awakening, are apt to lose the sense and impression of their first troubles for sin; but Providence is vigilant to prevent it, and doth effectually prevent it, sometimes by directing the minister to some discourse or passage that shall fall as pat as if the case of such a person had been studied by him, and designedly spoken to. How often have I found this in the cases of many souls, who have professed they have stood amazed to hear the very thoughts of their hearts discovered by the preacher, who knew nothing of them ! Sometimes by directing them to some proper rousing Scripture that suits their present case; and sometimes by suffering them to fall into some new sin, which shall awaken all their former troubles again, and put a new efficacy and activity into the conscience. The world is full of instances of all these cases, and because most Christians have experience of these things in themselves, it will be needless to recite them here. Search but a few years back, and you may remember that, according to this account, at least in some particulars, Providence ordered the matter with you. Have you not found some rod or other prepared by Providence to rouse you out of your security ? Why this is so common a thing with Christians, that they many times presage an affliction coming from the frames they find their own hearts in.

(2.) It gives also great assistance to the work of the Spirit upon the soul, by ordering, supporting, relieving, and cheering means, to prop up and comfort the soul, when it is overburdened, and ready to sink in the deeps of troubles. I remember Mr. Bolton gives us one instance which fits both these cases, the reviving of convictions, and seasonable supports in the deeps of troubles; and it is of a person that, by convictions, had been fetched off from his wicked companions, and entered into a reformed course of life; but after this, through the enticement of his old companions, the subtlety of Satan, and corruption of his own heart, did again relapse into the ways of sin: then was providentially brought to his view that Scripture, Prov. i. 24—26, &c.: this renewed his trouble, yea, aggravated it to a greater height than ever, insomuch that he could scarcely think, as it seems by the relation, his sin could be pardoned. But, in this plunge, the following text was presented to him, which sweetly settled him in a sure and glorious peace. "And if he trespass against thee seven times in a day, and seven times in a day turn again to thee, saying, I repent; thou shalt forgive him," Luke xvii. 4.

Nor can we here forget that miraculous work of Providence, in a time of great extremity, which was wrought for that good gentlewoman, Mrs. Honeywood, and is somewhere mentioned by the same author, who, under a deep and sad desertion, refused and put off all comfort, seeming to despair utterly of the grace and mercy of God. A worthy minister being one day with her, and reasoning against her desperate conclusions, she took a Venice glass from the table, and said, Sir, I am as sure to be damned as this glass is to be broken, and therewith threw it forcibly to the ground; but, to the astonishment of both, the glass remained whole and sound, which the minister taking up with admiration, rebuked her presumption, and showed her what a wonder Providence had wrought for her satisfaction, and it greatly

altered the temper of her mind. "O how unsearchable are his judgments! and his ways past
finding out!" Rom. xi. 33. "Lo! these are parts
of his ways; but how small a portion do we know
of him!" Job xxvi. 14.

And now suffer me to expostulate a little with
thy soul, reader. Hast thou been duly sensible of
thy obligation to Providence for this inestimable
favour? O what hath it done for thee! there
are divers kinds of mercies conveyed to men by
the hand of Providence, but none like this; in all
the treasury of his benefits, none is found like this.
Did it cast thee into the way of conversion, and
order the means and occasions of it for thee, when
thou little thoughest of any such thing? How
dear and sweet should the remembrance of it be to
thy soul! Methinks it should astonish and melt
you every time you reflect upon it. Such mercies
should never grow stale, or look like common
things to you: for, do but consider the following
particulars:

[1.] How surprising the mercy was which it
performed for you in that day. Providence had
a design upon you for your eternal good, which
you understood not. The time of mercy was now
fully come; the decree was now ready to bring
forth that mercy with which it had gone big from
eternity; and its gracious design must be executed
by the hand of Providence, so far as concerned the
external means and instruments; and how aptly
did it cause all things to fall in with that design,
though you knew not the meaning of it! Look
over all the before-mentioned examples, and you
shall see the blessed work of conversion begun
upon those souls, when they minded it no more
than Saul did a kingdom that morning he went out

to seek his father's asses, 1 Sam. ix. 3, 20.   Providence might truly have said to you in that day, as Christ said to Peter, " What I do thou knowest not now, but hereafter thou shalt know it," John xiii. 7.   " God's thoughts are not as our thoughts ; but, as the heavens are higher than the earth, so are his thoughts higher than ours, and his ways than our ways," Isa. lv. 8, 9.   Little did Zaccheus think, when he climbed up into the sycamore tree to see Christ as he passed that way, what a design of mercy Christ had upon him, who took thence the occasion of becoming both his guest and Saviour, Luke xix. 5—10.   And as little did some of you think, what the aim of Providence was when you went, some out of custom, others out of curiosity, if not worse ends, to hear such a sermon.   O how stupendous are the ways of God !

[2.] What a distinguishing and seasonable mercy was ushered in by Providence on that day.   It brought you to the means of salvation in a good hour.   At that very point of time, when the angel troubled the waters, you were brought to the pool ; to allude to that, John v. 4.   Now the accepted day was come, the Spirit was in the ordinance or providence, that converted you, and you were set in the way of it.   It may be, you had heard many hundred sermons before, but nothing would stick till now, because the hour was not come.   The Lord did as it were, call in the word for such a man, such a woman ; and Providence said, Lord, here he is ! I have brought him before thee ! There were many others under that sermon, who received no such mercy.   You yourselves had heard many before, but not to that advantage, as it is said, Luke iv. 27; " There were many lepers

in Israel in the days of Eliseus, but to none of
them was the prophet sent, save unto Naaman, the
Syrian." So there were many poor, unconverted
souls besides you under the word that day, and it
may be, to none of them was salvation sent that
day but to you. O blessed Providence, that set
you in the way of mercy at that time!

What a weighty and important mercy was pro-
videntally directed to your souls that day. There
are mercies of all sizes and kinds, in the hands of
Providence, to dispense to the sons of men: its
left hand is full of blessing, as well as its right.
It hath health and riches, honours and pleasures,
as well as Christ and salvation, to dispense. The
world is full of its left-hand favours; but the blessings of its right-hand are invaluably precious, and
few there be that receive them. It doth thousands
of kind offices for men; but among them all, this
is the chief—to lead and direct them to Christ.
For, consider, 1. Of all mercies this comes through
most and greatest difficulties, Eph. i. 19, 20.
2. This is a spiritual mercy, excelling, in dignity
of nature, all others, more than gold excels the dirt
under your feet, Rev. iii. 18. One such gift is
worth thousands of other mercies. 3. This is a
mercy immediately flowing out of the fountain of
God's electing love, a mercy never dropped into
any but an elect vessel, 1 Thess. i. 4, 5. 4. This
is a mercy that infallibly secures salvation; for, as
we may argue from conversion to election, looking
back; so from conversion to salvation, looking
forward, Heb. vi. 9. 5. This is an eternal mercy,
that which will stick by you when your father,
mother, wife, children, estate, honour, health, and
life shall fail you, John iv. 14.

O, therefore, set a special mark upon that providence that set you in the way of this mercy. It hath performed that for thee, which all the ministers on earth and angels in heaven could never have performed. This is a mercy that puts weight and value into the smallest circumstance that relates to it.

V. Thus you hear how instrumental Providence hath been in ordering the means and occasions of the greatest mercies for your souls. Let us now take into consideration another excellent performance of Providence, respecting the good of your bodies and souls too, in respect of that employment and calling, it ordered for you in this world; for it hath not only an eye upon your well-being in the world to come, but upon your well-being in this world also, and that very much depends upon the station and vocation to which it calls you.

Now, the providence of God, with respect to our worldly callings, may be displayed very takingly in the following particulars.

1. In directing you to a calling in your youth, and not suffering you to live an idle, useless, and sinful life, as many do, who are but burthens to the earth, the wens of the body politic, serving only to disfigure and drain it, to eat what others earn. Sin brought in sweat, Gen. iii. 19. But now not to sweat increaseth sin, 2 Thess. iii. 12. He that lives idly, cannot live honestly, as is plainly enough intimated, 1 Thess. iv. 11, 12. But when God puts men into a lawful calling, wherein the labour of their hands or heads is sufficient for them, it is a very valuable mercy, for thereby they eat their own bread, 2 Thess. iii. 12. Many a sad temptation is happily prevented; and they are ordinarily furnished by it for works of mercy to others: and surely it is more blessed to give than to receive.

7

2. In ordering you to such callings and employments, in the world, as are not only lawful in themselves, but most suitable to you. There be many persons employed in sinful trades and arts, merely to furnish other men's lusts: they do not only sin in their employments, but their very employments are sinful; they trade for hell, and are factors for the devil. Demetrius and the craftsmen of Ephesus got their estates by making shrines for Diana, Acts xix. 24, 25; that is, little cases or boxes, with folding leaves, within which the image of that idol sat enshrined. These were carried about by the people in procession, in honour of their idol. And at this day, how many wicked arts and employments are there invented, and multitudes of persons maintained by them, merely to gratify the pride and wantonness of a debauched age!

Now, to have an honest, lawful employment, wherein you do not dishonour God in benefitting yourselves, is no small mercy. But if it be not only lawful in itself, but suited to your genius and strength, there is a double mercy in it. Some poor creatures are engaged in callings that eat up their time and strength, and make their lives very uncomfortable to them: they have not only spending and wasting employments in the world, but such as allow little or no time for their general calling; and yet all this doth but keep them and theirs alive. Therefore, if God hath fitted you with an honest employment, wherein you have less toil than others, and more time for heavenly exercises, ascribe this benefit to the special care of Providence for you.

3. In settling you in such an employment and calling in the world, as possibly neither you nor your parents could ever expect you should ever arrive at. There are among us such persons as, on

this account, are signally obliged to divine Providence. God hath put them into such a way, as
neither they nor their parents ever projected. For,
look, as the needle in the compass turns now this
way, then that way, and never ceases moving till
it settle to the north point, just so it is in our settle-
ments in this world. A child is now designed for
this, then for that, but at last settles in that way of
employment which Providence designed him to.
How strangely are things wheeled about by Providence! Not what we, or our parents, but what
God designed shall take place. Amos was very
meanly employed at first, but God designed him
for a more honourable and comfortable calling,
Amos vii. 14, 15. David followed the ewes, and
likely never raised his thoughts to higher things in
the days of his youth; but God made him the royal
shepherd of a better flock, Psal. lxxviii. 70, 71.
Peter and Andrew were employed as fishermen,
but Christ called them from that to a higher calling,
to be fishers of men, Matt. iv. 18, 19. Pareus,
when he was fourteen years old, was, by the in-
stigation of his step-mother, placed with an apothe-
cary; but Providence so wrought that he was taken
off from that, and fitted for the ministry, wherein
he became a fruitful and eminent instrument to the
church. James Andreas was, by reason of his
father's inability to keep him at school, designed
for a carpenter; but was afterwards, by the per-
suasion of his friends, and assistance of the church
stock, sent to Stutgard, and thence to the univer-
sity, and so arrived at a very eminent station of
service in the church. A master builder, Œcolam-
padius, was, by his father, designed for a merchant;
but his mother, by earnest entreaties, prevailed to
keep him at school; and this man was a blessed

instrument in the reformation of religion. I might easily cite multitudes of such instances, but a few specimens may suffice.

4. In securing your estates from ruin, "Hast thou not made an hedge about him, and all that he hath?" Job i. 10. This is the inclosure of Providence, which secures to us what, by its favour, we acquire in the way of honest industry.

5. In making your calling sufficient for you. It was the prayer of Moses for the tribe of Judah, "Let his hands be sufficient for him," Deut. xxxiii. 7, and it is no small mercy if yours be so to you. Some there be that have work, but not strength to go through with it; others have strength, but no employment for it: some have hands and work for them, but it is not sufficient for them and theirs. If God bless your labour, so as to give you and yours necessary supports and comfort in the world by it, it is a choice providence, and with all thankfulness to be acknowledged.

If any that fear God should complain, that although they have a calling, yet it is a hard, laborious one, which takes up too much of their time, which they would gladly employ in other and better work, I answer, 1. It is likely the wisdom of Providence foresaw this to be the most suitable and proper employment for you; and, if you had more ease and rest, you might have more temptations than now you have. The strength and time which are now taken up in your daily labours, wherein you serve God, might otherwise have been spent upon such lusts wherein you might have served the devil. 2. Hereby, it may be, your health is the better preserved, and natural refreshments made the sweeter to you: "The sleep of a labouring man is sweet to him, whether he eat little or much; but the abundance of the rich will not suffer him to sleep," Eccl. v. 12. 3. And as to the service of God, if your hearts be spiritual, you may enjoy much communion with God in your very employments, and you have some intervals and respites for that purpose. Have you not more spare hours than you employ to that end?

But you may complain, All my labour will scarcely suffice to procure me and mine the necessaries of life. I am kept short and low to what others are; and this is a sad affliction.

Though the wisdom of Providence hath ordered you a lower and poorer condition than others, yet, 1. Consider how many are lower than you in the world; you have but little of the world, yet others have less. Read the description of those persons, Job xxx. 4. &c. 2. If God hath given you but a small portion of the world, yet, if you be godly, he hath promised never to forsake you, Heb. xiii. 5. 3. Providence hath ordered that condition for you which is really best for your eternal good. If you had more of the world than you have, your heads and hearts might not be able to manage it to your advantage. A small boat must have but a narrow sail. You have not wanted hitherto the necessaries of life, and are commanded, " having food and raiment," though none of the finest, " to be therewith content." " A little, that a righteous man hath, is better than the riches of many wicked." Psal. xxxvii. 16; better in the acquisition, sweeter in the fruition, and more comfortable in the account.

Well then, if Providence hath so disposed of you all, that you can eat your own bread, and so advantageously directed some of you to employments, that afford not only necessaries for your-

7 *

selves and families, but an overplus for works of
mercy to others, and all this brought about for you
in a way you did not project, let God be owned
and honoured in this providence. Will you not
henceforth call him, " My Father, the Guide of
my youth?" as it is Jer. iii. 4. Surely it was the
Lord who guided you to settle as you did in those
days of your youth. You reap at this day, and
may to your last day, the fruits of those early providences in your youth.

Now see that you walk answerable to the obli-
gations of Providence in this particular; and see
to it in the fear of God, that you abuse not any
of those things to his dishonour, which it hath
wrought for your comfort. To prevent which I
will here drop a few needful cautions, and conclude
this particular.

(1.) Be not slothful and idle in your vocations.
It is said, Augustus, built an Apragmapolis, a city void
of business; but I am sure God never erected any
city, town, or family, to that end. The command
to Adam, Gen. iii. 19, no doubt reaches all his
posterity; and gospel-commands back and second
it upon Christians. " Not slothful in business,"
Rom. xii. 11, and 2 Thess. iii. 11. If you be
negligent, you cannot be innocent. And yet,

(2.) Be not so intent upon your particular callings as to make them interfere with your general
calling. Beware you lose not your God in the
crowd and hurry of earthly business. Mind that
solemn warning, " But they that will be rich, fall
into temptation, and a snare, and into many foolish
and hurtful lusts, which drown men in destruction
and perdition," 1 Tim. vi. 9. The inhabitants of
Œnone, a dry island, near Athens, bestowed much
labour to draw in a river to water it, and make it

fruitful; but, when the sluices were opened, the waters flowed so abundantly, that it overflowed the island, and drowned the inhabitants. The application is obvious. It was an excellent saying of Seneca, I do not give, but lend myself to business.

(3.) Remember, always, that the success of your callings and earthly employments is, by the divine blessing, not human diligence alone. "Thou shalt remember the Lord thy God; for it is he that gave thee power to get wealth," Deut. viii. 18. The devil himself was so far orthodox as to acknowledge it: "Hast thou not made an hedge about him, and about his house, and about all that he hath on every side? Thou hast blessed the work of his hands," &c. Job i. 10. Recommend, therefore, your affairs to God by prayer: "Delight thyself also in the Lord, and he shall give thee the desires of thine heart. Commit thy way unto the Lord; trust also in him, and he shall bring it to pass," Psal. xxxvii. 4, 5, and touch not that which you cannot recommend to God by prayer for a blessing.

(4.) Be well satisfied in that station and employment in which Providence hath placed you, and do not so much as wish yourselves in another. "Let every man abide in the same calling wherein he was called," 1 Cor. vii. 20. Providence is wiser than you, and you may be confident hath suited all things better to your eternal good than you could do, had you been left to your own option.

VI. Thus you see the care Providence hath had over you in your youth, in respect to that worldly employment to which it guided you in .nose days.

We will, in the next place, consider it as our

guide, and the orderer of our relations for us. That Providence hath a special hand in this matter, is evident, both from Scripture assertions, and the acknowledgments of holy men, who, in that great concern of their lives, have still owned and acknowledged the directing hand of Providence. Take an instance of both. The Scripture plainly asserts the dominion of Providence over this affair. "A prudent wife is from the Lord," Prov. xix. 14, and "Whoso findeth a wife, findeth a good thing, and obtaineth favour of the Lord;" Prov. xviii. 22. So for children, "Lo, children are an heritage of the Lord; and the fruit of the womb is his reward," Psal. cxxvii. 3.

It hath ever been the practice of holy men to seek the Lord, for direction and counsel, when they have been upon the change of their condition. No doubt Abraham's encouragement in that case was the fruit of prayer, Gen. xxiv. 7. His pious servant also, who was employed in that affair, did both earnestly seek counsel of God, ver. 12, and thankfully acknowledged his gracious providence in guiding it, ver. 26, 27.

The same we may observe in children, the fruit of marriage, 1 Sam. i. 20, and Luke i. 13, 14. Now the providence of God may be divers ways displayed for the engaging of our hearts in love to the God of our mercies.

1. There is very much of Providence seen in appointing the parties for each other. In this the Lord goes oftentimes beyond our thoughts and projections; yea, and oftentimes crosses men's desires and designs to their great advantage. Not what they fancy, but what his infinite wisdom judges best and most beneficial for them, takes olace. Hence it is that probabilities are so often

dashed, and things remote, and utterly improbable, are brought about in very strange and unaccountable methods of Providence.

2. There is much of Providence seen in the harmony and agreeableness of tempers and dispositions ; from whence a very great part of the tranquillity and comforts of our lives results; or, at least, though natural tempers and educations did not so much harmonize before, yet they did so after they came under the ordinance of God ; "They two shall be one flesh," Gen. ii. 24, not one only in respect of God's institution, but one in respect of love and affection, that those who so lately were mere strangers to each other are now endeared to a degree beyond the nearest relations in blood as above. "For this cause shall a man leave father and mother, and shall cleave to his wife, and they two shall be one flesh," Matt. xix. 5.

3. But especially Providence is remarkable in making one instrumental to the eternal good of the other. "How knowest thou, O wife, but thou mayest save thy husband? or, how knowest thou, O man, whether thou shalt save thy wife?" 1 Cor. vii. 16. Hence is that grave exhortation to the wives of unbelieving husbands, 1 Pet. iii. 1, to win them by their conversation, which should be to them instead of an ordinance.

Or, if both be gracious, then what singular assistance and mutual help is hereby gained to the furtherance of their eternal good! While they live together "as heirs of the grace of life," 1 Pet. iii. 7. O blessed Providence, that directed such into so intimate relation on earth, who shall inherit together the common salvation in heaven!

4. How much of Providence is seen in children, the fruit of marriage! To have any posterity in

the earth, and not be left altogether as a dry tree;
to have comfort and joy in them, is a special providence, importing a special mercy to us. To
have the breaches made upon our families re-
paired, is a providence to be owned with a thankful heart; when God shall say to a man, as he
speaks, in another case, to the church, "The
children which thou shalt have, after thou hast
lost the other, shall say again in thine ears, The
place is too strait for me," &c. Isa. xlix. 20.

And these providences will appear more affectingly sweet and lovely to you, if you but compare
its allotments to you with what it hath allotted to
many others in the world. For, do but look
abroad, and you shall find multitudes unequally
yoked, to the embittering of their lives, whose relations are clogs and hinderances, both in temporals and spirituals; yea, we find an account in
Scripture of gracious persons, a great part of
whose comfort, in this world, hath been split
upon this rock. Abigail was a discreet and vir-
tuous woman, but very unsuitably matched to the
churlish Nabal, 1 Sam. xxv. 25. What a temptation to the neglect of a known duty prevailed upon
the renowned Moses, by the means of Zipporah
his wife! Exod. iv. 24, 25. David had his scoffing Michal, 2 Sam. vi. 20. And patient Job had
no small addition to all his other afflictions from
the wife of his bosom, who should have been a
support to him in the day of his trouble, Job xix.
17.

No doubt God sanctifies such rods to his people's good. If Socrates knew how to improve his
afflictions in his Xantippe, to the increase of his
patience, much more will they who converse with
God, under all providences, whether sweet or bit-

THE MYSTERY OF PROVIDENCE.   83

ter. Nevertheless, this must be acknowledged to
be a sad stroke upon any person, and such as
maims them upon the working hand, by unfitting
them for duty, 1 Pet. iii. 7, and cuts off much of
the comforts of life also.

How many are there who never enjoy the com-
·ortable fruits of marriage, but are denied the sight,
or at least the enjoyment of children! "Thus
saith the Lord, Write this man childless," &c.
Jer. xxii. 30, or, if they have children, yet cannot
enjoy them. "Though they bring up children,
yet will I bereave them, that there shall not be a
man left," Hos. ix. 12. They only bear for the
grave, and have their expectations raised to produce a greater affliction to themselves.

And it is no rare or unusual thing to see children and near relations the greatest instruments of
affliction to their parents and friends : so that, after
all their other sorrows and troubles in the world,
nearest relations bring up the rear of sorrows, as
one speaks, and prove greater griefs than any
other. O, how many parents have complained,
with the tree in the fable, that their very hearts
have been torn asunder with those wedges that
were cut out of their own bodies! What a grief
was Esau to Isaac and Rebecca! Gen. xxvi, 34,
35. What a scourge were Absalom and Amnon
to David!

Well, then, if God hath set the solitary in families, as it is in Psal. lxviii. 6, built a house for the
desolate, given you comfortable relations, which
are springs of daily comfort and refreshment to
you, you are, upon many accounts, engaged to
walk answerably to these gracious providences.
And that you may understand wherein that de-
corum and agreeable deportment with these provi-

dences consist, take up the sense of your duty in these brief hints:

1. Ascribe to God the glory of all those providential works which yield you comfort. You see a wise, directing, governing Providence, which hath disposed and ordered all things beyond your own projections and designs. "The way of man is not in himself, nor is it in him that walketh to direct his own steps," Jer. x. 23. Not what you projected, but what a higher counsel than yours determined, is come to pass. Good Jacob, when God had made him the father of a family, admired God in the mercy. "With my staff," said he, "I passed over this Jordan, and now I am become two bands," Gen. xxxii. 10. And how doth this mercy humble and melt him! "I am not worthy of the least of all the mercies, and of all the truth which thou hast showed unto thy servant."

2. Be exact in discharging the duties of those relations which so gracious a Providence hath led you into. Abuse not the effects of so much mercy and love to you. The Lord expects praise wherever you have comfort. This aggravated David's sin, that he should dare to abuse such great love and mercy as God had shown him in his family relations, 2 Sam. xii. 7—9.

3. Improve relations to the end Providence designed them. Walk together as co-heirs of the grace of life; study to be mutual blessings to each other; so walk in your relations, that the parting day may be sweet. Death will shortly break up the family; and then, nothing but the sense of duty discharged, or the neglects pardoned, will give comfort.

VII. You have heard how well Providence hath performed its part for you, in planting you into families who once were solitary. Now let us, in the next place, view another gracious performance of Providence for us, in making provision, from time to time, for us and our families. I the rather put these providences together in this place, because I find the Scripture doth so: " He setteth the poor on high from affliction, and maketh him families like a flock," Psal. cvii. 41.

You know the promises God hath made to his people ; " The young lions shall lack, and suffer hunger; but they that seek the Lord shall not want any good thing," Psal. xxxiv. 10. And have you not also seen the constant performance of it? Cannot you give the same answer, if the same question were propounded to you, that the disciples did, " Since I sent you forth, lacked ye any thing? and they said, Nothing," Luke xxii. 35. Can you not, with Jacob, call him " The God that fed you all your life long?" Gen. xlviii. Surely, " he hath given bread to them that fear him, and been ever mindful of his covenant," Psal. cxi. 5.

To display this providence, we will consider it in the following particulars :

1. The assiduity and constancy of the care of Providence for the saints. " His mercies are new every morning," Lam. iii. 23. It is not the supply of one or two pressing needs, but all your wants, as they grow from day to day, through all your days: " The God that fed me all my life long," Gen. xlviii. 15. The care of Providence runs parallel with the line of life. " Hearken unto me, O house of Jacob! and all the remnant of the house of Israel, which are borne by me from the belly, which are carried from the womb : and even to your old age I am he, and even to hoary hairs

8

will I carry you: I have made, and I will bear, even I will carry, and will deliver you," Isa. xlvi. 3, 4. So that, as God bid Israel "to remember from Shittim unto Gilgal, that they might know the faithfulness of the Lord," Mic. vi. 5, so would I persuade thee, reader, to record the ways of Providence, from first to last, throughout thy whole course to this day, that thou mayest see what a God he hath been to thee.

2. The seasonableness and opportunities of its provisions for them; for so runs the promise: " When the poor and needy seek water, and there is none, and their tongue faileth for thirst, I the Lord will hear them, I the God of Israel will not forsake them," Isa. xli. 17, and so hath the performance of it been. And this hath been made good to distressed saints sometimes in a more ordinary way, God secretly blessing a little, and making it sufficient for us and ours. Job tells us of " the secret of God upon his tabernacle," Job xxix. 4, that is, his secret blessing is in their tabernacles, by reason whereof it is that they subsist; but it is in an unaccountable way that they do so. Sometimes in an extraordinary way it breaks forth for their supply; so you find in 1 Kings xvii. 9—14. The cruse and barrel fail not.

Mr. Samuel Clark, in the life of that painful and humble servant of Christ, Mr. John Fox, records a memorable instance of Providence, and it is this: That towards the end of the reign of Henry VIII. he went to London, where he quickly spent that little his friends had given him, or he had acquired by his own diligence, and began to be in great want. As one day he sat in St. Paul's church, spent with long fasting, his countenance thin, and his eyes hollow, after the ghastly manner of dying

men, every one shunning a spectacle of so much
horror, there came one to him whom he had never
seen before, and thrust an untold sum of money
into his hand, bidding him be of good cheer, and
accept that small gift in good part from his coun-
tryman; and that he should make much of himself, for that, within a few days, new hopes were
at hand, and a more certain condition of livelihood.
Three days after, the duchess of Richmond sent
for him to live in her house, and to be tutor to the
earl of Surrey's children, then under her care.

Mr. Isaac Ambrose, a worthy divine, whose
labours have made him acceptable to his generation, in his epistle to the earl of Bedford, prefixed
to his " Last Things," gives a pregnant instance
in his own case. His words are these : " For
mine own part," saith he, " however the Lord
hath seen cause to give me but a poor pittance of
outward things, for which I bless his name ; yet,
in the income thereof, I have many times observed so much of his peculiar providence, that thereby they have been very much sweetened, and my
heart hath been raised to admire his grace. When,
of late, under a hard dispensation, which I judge
not meet to mention, wherein I suffered conscien-
tiously, all streams of wonted supplies being stopped, the waters of relief for myself and family did
run low, I went to bed with some staggerings
and doubtings of the fountain's letting out itself for
our refreshing ; but, ere I awoke in the morning,
a letter was brought to my bed-side, which was
signed by a choice friend, Mr. Anthony Ash,
which reported some unexpected breakings-out of
God's goodness for my comfort. These are some
of his lines : ' Your God, who hath given you a
heart thankfully to record your experiences of his

goodness, doth renew experiences for your encouragement. Now I shall report one which will
raise your spirit toward the God of your mercies.'
Whereupon he sweetly concludes, One morsel of
God's provision, especially when it comes in unexpectedly, and upon prayer, when wants are
most, will be more sweet to spiritual relish, than
all former enjoyments were."

3. The wisdom of Providence in our provision.
And this is discovered in two things: 1. In pro-
portioning the quantity, not satisfying our extra-
vagant wishes, but answering our real needs: consulting our wants, not our wantonness: " My God
shall supply all our wants," Phil. iv. 19, and this
hath exactly suited the wishes of the best and
wisest men, who desired no more at his hands. So
Jacob, Gen. xxviii. 20, and Agur, Prov. xxx. 8, 9.
Wise Providence considers our conditions, as pil-
grims and strangers, and so allots the provision
that is needful for our passage home. It knows
the mischievous influence of fulness and redun-
dancy upon most men, though sanctified; and how
apt it is to make them remiss and forgetful of God,
Deut. vi. 12, that their hearts, like the moon, suffer an eclipse when it is at the full, and so suits
and orders all to their best advantage. 2. Its wisdom is much discovered in the manner of dispensing our portion to us. It many times suffers our
wants to pinch hard, and many fears to arise, out
of design to magnify the care and love of God in
the supply, Deut. viii. 3. Providence so orders
the case, that faith and prayer, coming between our
want and supplies, the goodness of God may be the
more magnified in our eyes thereby.

And now let me beg you to consider the good
hand of Providence, that hath provided for, and

suitably supplied you and yours all your days, and never failed you hitherto; and labour to walk suitably to your experiences of such mercies. In order whereunto, let me press a few suitable cautions upon you.

(1.) Beware that you forget not the care and kindness of Providence, which your eyes have seen in so many fruits and experiences thereof. It was God's charge against Israel, "That they soon forgot his wondrous works," Psal. cvi. 13. A bad heart and a slippery memory deprive men of the comfort of many mercies, and defraud God of the glory due for them.

(2.) Do not distrust Providence in future exigencies. Thus they did, "Behold, he smote the rock, that the waters gushed out, and the streams overflowed: can he give bread also? Can he provide flesh for his people? Psal. lxxviii. 20. How unreasonable and absurd are these queries of unbelief, especially after their eyes had seen the power of God in such extraordinary effects!

(3.) Do not murmur and regret under new straits. This is a vile temper; and yet how incident to us, when wants press hard upon us. Ah! did we but rightly understand what the demerit of sin is, we should rather admire the bounty of God, than complain of the strait-handedness of Providence; and if we did but consider that there lies upon God no obligation of justice or gratitude, to reward any of our duties, it would cure our murmurs.

(4.) Do not show the least discontent at the lot and portion Providence carves out to you. O that you would be well pleased and satisfied with all its appointments! Say, "The lines are fallen unto me in pleasant places; yea, I have a goodly heritage," Psal. xvi. 6. Surely that is best for you

8*

which Providence hath appointed, and, one day, you yourselves will judge it so to be.

(5.) Do not neglect when straits befall you. You see it is Providence dispenses all : you live upon it ; therefore apply yourselves to God in the times of need. This is evidently included in the promise, Isa. xli. 17, as well as expressed in the command, Phil. iv. 6. Remember God, and he will not forget you.

(6.) Do not distract your hearts with sinful cares, Matt. vi. 25, 26. Consider the fowls of the air, saith Christ ; not the fowls at the door, that are daily fed by hand, but those of the air, that know not where to have the next meal ; and yet God provides for them. Remember your relation to Christ, and his engagements by promise to you, and by these things work your hearts to satisfaction and content with all the allotments of Providence.

VIII. The next great advantage and mercy the saints receive from the hand of Providence, is in their preservation from the snares and temptations of sin, by its preventing care over them. That Providence wards off many a deadly stroke of temptation, and puts by many a mortal thrust which Satan makes at our souls, is a truth as manifest as the light that shineth. This is included in that promise, " God will with the temptation make a way to escape, that ye may be able to bear it," 1 Cor. x. 13. Providence gives an outlet for the soul's escape, when it is shut up into the dangerous straits of temptation. There are two eminent ways, whereby the force and efficacy of temptation is broken in believers. One is by the operation of internal grace, " The spirit lusteth against the flesh," Gal. v. 17, so that ye cannot do the things that ye would ; that is, sanctification destroys sin

after it hath been conceived in the soul.   The other
way is by the external working of Providence;
and of this I am here engaged to speak.

The Providence of God is the great hinderance
to a world of sin, which else would break forth,
like an overflowing flood, from our corrupt natures.
It prevents abundance of sin which else wicked
men would commit.   The men of Sodom were
greedily pursuing their lusts; God providentially
hindered it, by smiting them blind, Gen. xix. 11.
Jeroboam intended to smite the prophet; Providence interposed, and withered his arm, 1 Kings
xiii. 4.   Thus you see, when wicked men have
contrived, and are ready to execute their wickedness, Providence claps on its manacles, " that
their hands cannot perform their enterprises,"
Job v. 12.

And so much corruption there remains on good
men, that they would certainly plunge themselves
under much more guilt than they do, if Providence
did not take greater care of them than they do of
themselves; for though they make conscience of
keeping themselves, and daily watch their hearts
and ways, yet such is the deceitfulness of sin, that
if Providence did not lay blocks in their way, it
would, more frequently than it doth, entangle and
defile them.   And this it doth divers ways.

1. Sometimes by stirring up others to interpose
with seasonable counsels, which effectually dis-
suade them from prosecuting an evil design. Thus
Abigail meets David in the nick of time and dis-
suades him from his evil purpose, 1 Sam. xxv. 34.

And I find it recorded, as on another account
was noted before, of that holy man, Mr. Dod, that
being late at night in his study, he was strongly
moved (though at an unseasonable hour) to visit a

gentleman of his acquaintance; and not knowing what might be the design of Providence therein he obeyed and went. When he came to the house, after a few knocks at the door, the gentleman himself came to him, and asked him whether he had any business with him. Mr. Dod answered, No; but that he could not be quiet till he had seen him. O, sir, replied the gentleman, you are sent of God at this hour, for just now (and with that takes the halter out of his pocket) I was going to destroy myself. And thus was the mischief prevented.

2. Sometimes by hindering the means and instruments, whereby the evil itself is prevented. Thus, when good Jehoshaphat had joined himself with that wicked king Ahaziah to build ships at Ezion-Geber to go to Tarshish, God prevents the design by breaking the ships with a storm, as you read in 2 Chron. xx. 35–37.

We find also, in the life of Mr. Bolton, written by Mr. Bagshaw, that, while he was in Oxford, he had familiar acquaintance with Mr. Anderton, a good scholar, but a strong papist, who, knowing Mr. Bolton's good parts, and perceiving that he was in some outward wants, took this advantage, and used many arguments to persuade him to be reconciled to the church of Rome, and to go over with him to the English seminary, assuring him he should be furnished with all necessaries, and have gold enough. Mr. Bolton being at that time poor in mind and purse, accepted the motion, and the day and place were appointed in Lancashire, where they should meet and take shipping, and be gone: but Mr. Anderton came not, and so he escaped the snare.

3. Sometimes, by laying some strong afflictions upon the body, to prevent a worse evil; and this

is the meaning of, " I will hedge up her way with thorns," Hos. ii. 6. Thus Basil was a long time exercised with a violent headache, which, as he observed, was used by Providence to prevent lust. Paul had a thorn in his flesh, a messenger of Satan sent to buffet him; and this affliction, whatever it was, was ordained to prevent pride in him, 2 Cor. xii. 7.

4. Sometimes sin is prevented in the saints by the better information of their minds, by the sacred oracles of God. Thus, when sinful motions began to rise in David's mind, from the prosperity of the wicked, and his own afflicted state, and grew to that height, that he began to think all he had done in the way of religion was little better than lost labour; he is set right again, and the temptation dissolved, by going into the sanctuary, where God showed him how to take new measures of persons and things; to judge of them by their ends and issues, not their present appearances, Psal. lxxiii. 12, 13, 17.

5. And sometimes the providence of God prevents the sins of his people by removing them out of the way of temptation by death! in which sense we may understand this text: " The righteous is taken away from the evil to come," Isa. lvii. 1, the evil of sin as well as sufferings. When the Lord sees his people low-spirited, and not able to grapple with strong trials and temptations, which are drawing on, it is, with respect to them, a providence to be disbanded by death, and set out of harm's way.

Now, consider and admire the providence of God, O ye saints, who hath had more care of your souls than ever ye had of them! Had not the providence of God thus wrought for you in a way of prevention, it may be you had this day been so many Magor Missabibs. Jer. xx. 3. How was the heart of David melted under that preventing providence before mentioned in 1 Sam. xxv. 34, he blessed the Lord, the instrument, and that counsel by which his soul was preserved from sin. Do but seriously bethink yourselves of a few particulars about this case ; as,

(1.) How your corrupt natures have often impetuously hurried you on toward sin, so that all the grace you had could not withstand its force, if Providence had not prevented it in some such method as you have heard. "Every man is tempted when he is drawn away of his own lusts, and enticed," James i. 14. You found yourselves but feathers in the wind of temptation.

(2.) How near you have been brought to the brink of sin, and yet saved by a merciful hand of Providence ! May you not say, "I was almost in the midst of all evils," Prov. v. 14 ; or, "My feet were almost gone, my steps had well nigh slipped," Psal. lxxiii. 2. O merciful Providence ! that stepped in so opportunely to your relief.

(3.) How many have been suffered to fall by the hand of temptations, to the reproach of religion, and wounding of their own conscience to that degree, that they have never recovered former peace again, but lived in the world devoid of comfort to their dying day !

(4.) How woful your case had been, if the Lord had not mercifully saved you from many thousand temptations which have assaulted you ! I tell you, you cannot estimate the mercies you possess by means of such providences. Are your names sweet, and your consciences peaceful ? Two mercies as dear to you as your two eyes. Why, surely you owe them, if not wholly, yet in a great measure, to the aids and assistances Providence hath given you all along the way you have passed, through the dangerous tempting world, to this day.

Walk, therefore, suitably to this obligation of Providence also, and see that you thankfully own it. Do not impute your escapes from sin to accidents, or to your own watchfulness or wisdom; yet see that you tempt not Providence, on the other hand, by an irregular reliance upon its care over you, without taking all due care of yourselves. "Keep yourselves in the love of God," Jude 21. "Keep your hearts with all diligence," Prov. iv 23. Though Providence keep you, yet it is in the way of your duty.

IX. Thus you see what care Providence hath had over your souls, in preventing the spiritual dangers and miseries that else would have befallen you in the way of temptations. In the next place, I will show you, that it hath been no less careful for your bodies, and with how great tenderness it hath carried them in its arms, through innumerable hazards and dangers also. "Thou keepest me as the apple of thine eye."* Psal. xvii. 8. He is called "the Keeper of Israel, that never slumbereth nor sleepeth," Psal. cxxi. 4; "the Preserver of men," Job vii. 20.

To display the glory of his providence before

---

* The eye hath five tunics to guard it against danger. The first is like a spider's web; the second is like a net; the third is like a berry; the fourth is like a horn; and the fifth is the cover or lid of the eye. Here is guard upon guard, resembling the various ways Providence hath to secure us from ruin.

you, let us take into consideration the perils into
which the best of men sometimes fall, and the
ways and means by which Providence preserves
them in those dangers.

There are manifold hazards into which we are
often cast in this world. The apostle Paul gives
us a general account of his dangers in 2 Cor. xi.
26. And how great a wonder is it, that our lives
have not been extinguished in some of those dangers we have been in! For, 1. Have not some of
us fallen, and that often, into very dangerous sicknesses and diseases; in which we have approached
to the very brink of the grave? and have, or
might have said with Hezekiah, "I said in the
cutting off of my days, I shall go to the gates of
the grave: I am deprived of the residue of my
years," Isa. xxxviii. 10. Have we not often had
the sentence of death in ourselves; and our bodies
at that time been like a leaky ship in a storm, that
hath taken in water on every side till it was ready
to sink? Yet hath God preserved, careened, and
launched us out again as well as ever. O! what
a wonder is it that such a crazy body should be
preserved for so many years, and survive so many
dangers! Surely it is not more admirable to see
a Venice glass pass from hand to hand, in continual use, for forty or fifty years, and still to re-
main whole, notwithstanding many knocks, and
falls it hath had. If you enjoy health, or recover
out of sickness, it is because " he puts none of
those diseases upon thee," or, because he is " the
Lord thy physician," Exod. xv. 26.

2. And how many deadly dangers hath his
hand rescued some of you from, in those years of
confusion and public calamity, when the sword
was bathed in blood, and made horrid slaughter,

when, it may be, your lives were often given you
for a prey! This David put a special remark
upon: "O God the Lord, the strength of my salvation, thou hast covered my head in the day of
battle," Psal. cxl. 7.

Beza, being in France in the first civil war, and
there tossed up and down for twenty-two months,
recorded six hundred deliverances from dangers in
that space, for which he solemnly gave God thanks
in his last testament. If the sword destroyed you
not, it was because God did not give it a commission so to do.

3. Many of you have seen wonders of salvation
upon the deeps, where the hand of God hath been
signally stretched forth for your rescue and deliverance. This is elegantly expressed in Psal. cvii.
23—27; concerning which you may say, in a
proper sense, what the Psalmist doth metaphori-
cally, "If it had not been the Lord who was on
our side, then the waters had overwhelmed us,
the streams had gone over our soul," Psal. cxxiv.
1, 4. To see men who have spent so many years
upon the seas, where your lives have continually
hung in suspense before you, attain to your years,
when you could neither be reckoned among the
living nor the dead, as seamen are not, O! what
cause have you to adore your great Preserver!
Many thousands of your companions are gone
down, and you yet here to praise the Lord, among
the living. You have bordered nearer to eternity
all your days than others, and often been in imminent perils upon the seas. Surely such, and so
many salvations, call aloud upon you for most
thankful acknowledgments.

4. To conclude: How innumerable hazards and
accidents, the least of which have cut off others,

9

hath God carried us all through! I think I may
safely say, your primitive and positive mercies, of
this kind, are more in number than the hairs of
your heads.   Many thousands of these dangers
we never saw, nor were made particularly sensible
of; but though we saw them not, our God did
and brought us out of danger, before he brought us
into fear.   Some have been evident to us, and
those so remarkable, that we cannot think or speak
of them to this day but our souls are freshly affected
with those mercies.

It is recorded of our famous Jewell, that about
the beginning of Queen Mary's reign, the Inquisi-
tion, taking hold of him in Oxford, he fled to London by night; but providentially losing the road,
he escaped the inquisitors, who pursued him.
However, he fell that night into another imminent
hazard of life, for, wandering up and down in the
snow, he fainted, and lay starving in the way,
panting and labouring for life, at which time Mr.
Latimer's servant found and saved him.

It were easy to multiply examples of this kind,
histories abounding with them; but I think there
are few of us but are furnished out of our own experience abundantly; so that I shall rather choose
to press home the sense of these providences upon
you, in order to a suitable return to the God of
your mercies for them, than add more instances of
this kind.   To this purpose, I desire you seriously
to weigh the following particulars:

(1.) Consider what you owe to Providence for
your protection, by which your life hath been pro-
tracted unto this day, with the usefulness and comfort thereof.   Look abroad in the world, and you
may daily see some in every place, who are objects of pity, bereaved by sad accidents of all the

comforts of life, whilst, in the mean time, Providence hath tenderly preserved you, " keeping all your bones, so that none of them is broken," Psal. xxxiv. 20. Is the elegant and comely structure of thy body not spoiled, thy members not distorted, and made so many seats of torment, the usefulness of any part not destroyed ? Why, this is because Providence never quitted his hold of thee since thou camest out of the womb, but, with a watchful eye and tender hand, hath guarded thee in every place, and kept thee as its charge.

(2.) Consider how every member, which hath been so tenderly kept, hath, nevertheless, been an instrument of sin against the Lord, and that not only in the days of your unregeneracy, when, " ye yielded your members as instruments of unrighteousness unto sin," Rom. vi. 13, but ever since you gave them up in covenant unto the Lord as dedicated instruments to his service ; and yet how tender hath Providence been over them ! You have often provoked him to afflict you in every part, and lay penal evil upon every member that hath been instrumental in moral evil; but O how great have his compassions been towards you, and his patience admirable !

(3.) Consider what is the aim of Providence, in all the tender care it hath manifested for you. Why doth it protect you so assiduously, and suffer no evil to befall you? Is it not that you should employ your bodies for God, and cheerfully apply yourselves to that service he hath called you to ? Doubtless this is the end and level of these mercies ; for, else, to what purpose are they afforded you ? Your bodies are a part of Christ's purchase, as well as your souls, 1 Cor. vi. 19; they are committed to the charge and tutelage of angels, Heb. i.

14, who have performed many services for them.
They are dedicated by yourselves to the Lord, and
that upon the highest account, Rom. xii. 1. They
have already been the subjects of manifold mercies
in this world, Psal. xxxv. 10, and shall partake of
singular glory and happiness in the world to come,
Phil. iii. 21. And shall they not be employed,
yea, cheerfully worn out in his service? How reasonable is it they should be so! Why are they so
tenderly preserved by God, if they must not be
used for God?

X. You have heard of many great things performed for you by Divine Providence in the former
particulars; but there is an eminent favour it bestows on the saints, which hath not yet been considered, and indeed is too little minded by us, and
that is, the aid and assistance it gives the people of
God in the great work of mortification.

Mortification of our sinful affections and passions
is the one-half of our sanctification; "Dead indeed
unto sin, but alive unto God," Rom. vi. 11. It is
the great evidence of our interest in Christ. See
Gal. v. 24; Rom. vi. 5—9. It is our safety in
the hour of temptation. The corruptions in the
world are through lust, 2 Pet. i. 4. Our instrumental fitness for service depends much upon it,
2 Tim. ii. 21; John xv. 2. How great a service
to our souls, therefore, must that be by which this
blessed work is carried on upon them!

Now, there are two means or instruments employed in this work. The Spirit who effects it
internally, Rom. viii. 13, and Providence, which
assists it externally. The Spirit indeed is the
principal agent, upon whose operation the success
of this work depends; and all the providences in
the world can never effect it without him. But

these are secondary and subordinate means, which, by the blessing of the Spirit upon them, have a great efficacy in the work. How they are so serviceable to this end and purpose, I shall open in the following account.

1. More generally. The most wise God orders the dispensations of Providence in a blessed subordination to the work of his Spirit. There is a sweet harmony between them in their distinct workings. They all meet in that one blessed issue which God hath by the counsel of his will directed them to, Eph. i. 11, and Rom. viii. 28. Hence it is that the Spirit is said to be in, and to order the motions of, the wheels of Providence, Ezek. i. 20, and so they move together by consent. Now, one great part of the Spirit's internal work being to destroy sin in the people of God, see how conformable to his design external providences are steered and ordered, in the following particulars.

There is in all the regenerate, a strong propensity and inclination to sin, and in that lies a principal part of the power of sin. Of this Paul sadly complains: " But I see another law in my members, warring against the law of my mind, and bringing me into captivity to the law of sin, which is in my members," Rom. vii. 23. And every believer daily finds it to his grief. O it is hard to forbear those things that grieve God! God hath made a hedge about us, and fenced us against sin by his laws; but there is a proneness in nature to break over the hedge, and that against the very resistance of the Spirit of God in us. Now see, in this case, the concurrence and assistance of Providence for the prevention of sin; look, as the Spirit internally resists those sinful inclinations, so Providence externally lays bars and blocks in our

way to hinder and prevent sin. And this is the
meaning of those places lately cited, Hos. ii. 6,
and 2 Cor. xii. 7. So Job xxxiii. 17—19. There
is many a bodily distemper inflicted on this very
score, to be a clog to prevent sin! O bear them
patiently upon this consideration.

Basil was sorely grieved with an inveterate
headache; he earnestly prayed that it might be
removed. But no sooner was he freed of this
clog, but he felt the inordinate motions of lust;
which made him pray for his headache again. So
it might be with many of us, if our clogs were
cut off.

A question may be moved here, whether it be
the genius and property of a gracious spirit to forbear sin, because of the rod of affliction. They
have surely higher motives and nobler principles
than these. This is the temper of a carnal and
slavish spirit. Indeed it is so when this is the sole
or principal restraint from sin; when a man abhors
not sin, because of the intrinsic filth, but only because of the troublesome consequences and effects.
But this is vastly different from the case of the
saints under sanctified afflictions; for, as they have
higher motives and nobler principles, so they have
lower and more sensible ones too; and these are,
in their kind and place, very useful to them. Besides, you must know, that afflictions work in another way upon gracious hearts to restrain them
from sin, or warn them against sin, than they do
upon others. It is not so much the smart of the
rod which they feel, as the tokens of God's displeasure, which affright and scare them. "Thou
renewest thy witnesses against me," &c. Job x.
17, and this is that which principally affects them.
'O Lord, rebuke me not in thine anger, neither

chasten me in thy hot displeasure," Psal. vi. 1,
and " O Lord, correct me, but with judgment, not
in thine anger, lest thou bring me to nothing,"
Jer. x. 24.   And surely this is no low and common argument.

2. Notwithstanding this double sense of God's
command and preventive afflictions, yet sin is too
hard for the best of men; their corruptions carry
them through all to sin: and when it is so, not
only doth the Spirit work internally, but Providence also works externally, in order to their
reduction.   The ways of sin are not only made
bitter unto them by the remorse of conscience, but
by those afflictive rods upon the outward man, with
which God also follows it; and, in both these respects I find that place expounded " Whoso break-
eth a hedge, a serpent shall bite him," Eccles. x.
8. If, as some expound it, the hedge be the law
of God, then the serpent is the remorse of conscience, and the sharp teeth of affliction, which he
shall quickly feel, if he be one that belongs to
God.

The design and aim of these afflictive providences is to purge and cleanse them from that pollution into which temptations have plunged them.
" By this shall the iniquity of Jacob be purged,
and this is all the fruit, to take away his sin," Isa.
xxvii. 9. To the same purpose is this passage,
"Before I was afflicted, I went astray; but now
have I kept thy word," Psal. cxix. 67.   These
afflictions have the same use and end to our souls
that frosty weather hath upon those clothes that
are laid a-bleaching; they alter the hue, and make
them whiter. "And some of them of understanding shall fail, to try them, and to purge, and to
make them white," Dan. xi. 35.

And here it may be queried, upon what account afflictions are said to purge away the iniquities of the saints. Is it not unwarrantable, and very dishonourable to Christ, to attribute that to affliction, which is the peculiar honour of his blood?

It is confessed, that the blood of Christ is the only lavatory, or fountain, opened for sin, and that no afflictions, howsoever many, or strong, or continual they be, can in themselves purge away the pollution of sin, as we see in wicked men, who are afflicted, and afflicted, and again afflicted, and yet nevertheless sinful; and the torments of hell, how extreme, universal, and continual soever they are, yet shall never fetch out the stain of one sin.

But yet this hinders not but that a sanctified affliction may, in the efficacy and virtue of Christ's blood, produce such blessed effects upon the soul. Though a cross, without a Christ, never did any man good; yet thousands have been beholden to the cross as it hath wrought in the virtue of his death for their good; and this is the case of those souls that this discourse is concerned about.

3. We find the best hearts, if God bestow any comfortable enjoyment upon them, too apt to be overheated in their affections towards it, and to be too much taken up with these outward comforts. This also shows the great power and strength of corruption in the people of God, and must, by some means or other, be mortified in them. This was the case of Hezekiah; his heart was too much affected with his treasures, so that he could not hide a vain-glorious temper, as you find in Isa. xxxix. 2; and so good David thought his mountain, that is, his kingdom, and the splendour and glory of his present state, had stood so fast that it should never be moved, Psal. xxx. 7. How did

the same good man let out his heart and affections upon his beautiful son Absalom! as appears by the doleful lamentation he made at his death, prizing him above his own life, which was a thousand times more worth than he. So Jonah, when God raised up a gourd for him to shelter him from the sun, how excessively was he taken with it, and was exceedingly glad of it!

But will God suffer things to lie thus? Shall the creature purloin and draw away our affections from him? No; this is our corruption, and God will purge it. And to this end he sends forth Providence to smite those creatures on which our affections are either inordinately or excessively let out, or else to turn them into rods, and smite us by them.

Is Hezekiah too much puffed up with his full exchequer? Why, those very Babylonians, to whom he boasted of it, shall empty it, and make a prey of it, Isa. xxxix. 6. Is David hugging himself in a fond conceit of the stability of his earthly splendour? Lo! how soon God beclouds all, Psal. xxx. 7. Is Absalom doated on, and has he crept too far into his good father's heart? This shall be the son of his sorrow, who shall seek after his father's life. Is Jonah so transported with his gourd? God will prepare a worm to smite it, Jonah iv. 6, 7.

How many husbands, wives, and children, hath Providence smitten upon this very account! God might have spared them longer, if they had been loved more regularly and moderately. This hath blasted many an estate and hopeful project, and it is a merciful dispensation for our good.

4. The strength of our unmortified corruption shows itself in our pride, and the swelling vanity

of our hearts, when we have a name and esteem among men, when we are applauded and honoured, when we are admired for any gift or excellency that is in us ; this draws forth the pride of the heart, and shows the vanity that is in it. So you read, " As the fining-pot for silver, and the furnace for gold, so is a man to his praise," Prov. xxvii. 21, that is, as the furnace will discover what dross is in the metal, when it is melted, so will praise and commendations discover what pride is in the heart of him that receives them. This made a good man say, " He that praises me, wounds me." And, which is more strange, this corruption may be felt in the heart, even when the last breath is ready to expire. It was a saying of one of the German divines, when those about him recounted, for his encouragement, the many services he had done for God : " Take away the fire, for there is still the chaff of pride in me." To crucify this corruption, Providence takes off the bridle of restraint from ungodly men, and sometimes permits them to traduce the names of God's servants, as Shimei did David's. Yea, they shall fall into disesteem among their friends, as Paul did among the Corinthians ; and all this to keep down the swelling of their spirits at the sense of those excellencies that are in them ; the design of these providences being nothing else than to hide pride from man. Yea, it deserves a special remark, that when some good men have been engaged in a public and eminent work, and have therein, it may be, too much sought their own applause, God hath withheld such usual assistance at such times from them, and caused them to falter so in their work, that they have come off with shame and pity at such times, how ready and self-possessed soever they have been at other times. It were easy to give divers remarkable examples to confirm this observation. But I pass on.

5. The corruption of the heart shows itself, in raising up great expectations to ourselves from the creature, and projecting abundance of felicity and contentment from some promising and hopeful enjoyments we have in the world. This we find to have been the case of holy Job in the days of his prosperity. " Then I said, I shall die in my nest, I shall multiply my days as the sand," Job xxix. 18. But how soon were all these expectations dashed by a gloomy providence, that benighted him in the noontide of his prosperity! And all this for his good, to take off his heart more fully from creature-expectations. We often find the best men to over-reckon themselves in worldly things, and over-act their confidences about them. They that have great and well-grounded expectations from heaven, may have too great and ungrounded expectations from the earth. But when it is so, it is very usual for Providence to undermine their earthly hopes, and convince them, by experience, how vain they are. Thus the people's hearts were intently set upon prosperous providences, full harvests, and great increase; whilst in the mean time, no regard was had to the worship of God, and the things of his house; therefore Providence blasts their hopes, and brings them to little, Haggai ii. 19.

Corruption discovers itself in dependence upon creature-comforts and sensible props. O! how apt are the best of men to lean upon those things and stay themselves upon them! Thus did Israel stay themselves upon Egypt, as a feeble man would lean upon his staff; but God suffered it both to fail them and wound them, Ezek. xxix. 6, 7. So how apt are individuals to depend upon their sensible supports! Thus we lean on our relations, and the inward thoughts of our hearts are, that they shall be to us so many springs of comfort to refresh us throughout our lives; but God will show us, by his providence, our mistake and error in these things. Thus a husband is smitten to draw the soul of a wife nearer to God in dependence upon him, 1 Tim. v. 5. So for children, we are apt to say of this or that child as Lamech did of Noah, " This same shall comfort us," Gen. v. 29, but the wind passes over these flowers, and they are withered, to teach us that our happiness is not bound up in these enjoyments. So for our estates, when the world smiles upon us, and we have got a warm nest, how do we prophesy of rest and peace in those acquisitions, minding, with good Baruch, great things for ourselves; but Providence, by a particular or general calamity, overturns our projects, as Jer. xlv. 4, 5, and all this to reduce our hearts from the creature to God, our only rest.

Corruption discovers its strength in good men, by their adherence to things below, and unwillingness to go hence. This often proceeds from the engaging enjoyments and pleasant fruitions we have here below. Providence mortifies this inclination in the saints by killing those ensnaring comforts before-hand, making all, or most of our pleasant things to die before us; by embittering this world to us by the troubles of it; and by making life undesirable, through the pains and infirmities we feel in the body, and so loosing our root, in order to our more easy fall by the fatal stroke.

And thus, I have furnished the second general head; but, before I pass from this, I cannot but make a pause, and desire you, with me, to stand in a holy amazement, and wonder at the dealings of God with such poor worms as we are! Surely God deals familiarly with men! His condescensions to his own clay are astonishing! All that I shall note at present about it shall be under these three heads, wherein I find the matter of my present meditations summed up by the Psalmist, "Lord, what is man that thou takest knowledge of him? or the son of man that thou makest account of him?" Psal. cxliv. 3.

In this Scripture you have represented the immense and transcendent greatness of God, who is infinitely above us and all our thoughts: "Canst thou by searching find out God? Canst thou find out the Almighty to perfection? It is as high as heaven, what canst thou do? deeper than hell, what canst thou know? the measure thereof is longer than the earth, and broader than the sea," Job xi. 7—9. "The heaven, and heaven of heavens cannot contain him," 2 Chron. ii. 6. "He is glorious in holiness, fearful in praises, doing wonders," Exod. xv. 11. When the Scriptures speak of him comparatively, see how it expresses his greatness: "Behold the nations are as the drop of a bucket, and are counted as the small dust of the balance; behold he taketh up the isles as a very little thing. And Lebanon is not sufficient to burn, nor the beasts thereof sufficient for a burnt-offering. All nations before him are as nothing, and they are accounted to him less than nothing, and vanity," Isa. xl. 15—17. When the holiest men have addressed themselves to him, see with what humility and deep adoration they have spoken of him and to him! "Woe is me, for I am undone, because I am a man of unclean lips, and I dwell in the midst of a people of unclean lips: for mine eyes have seen

10

the King, the Lord of hosts," Isa. vi. 5. Nay,
what respects the very angels of heaven have of
that glorious majesty, you may see, ver. 2, 3
" Each one had six wings, with twain he covered
his face, and with twain he covered his feet, and
with twain he did fly. And one cried to another,
and said, Holy, holy, holy is the Lord of hosts;
the whole earth is full of his glory."

Also here is shown the baseness, vileness, and
utter unworthiness of man, yea, the holiest and
best of men, before God. " Verily, every man at
his best estate, is altogether vanity," Psal. xxxix.
5. Every man, take where you will, and every
man, in his best estate, or standing in his freshest
glory, is not only vanity, but altogether vanity, or
every man is very vanity; for do but consider the
best of men in their extraction, in their constitution, and in their outward condition. In their extraction, " by nature children of wrath, even as
others," Eph. iii. 3. The blood that runs in our
veins is as much tainted as theirs in hell. Consider them in their constitution, and natural temper, and it is no better: yea, in many a worse
temper than in reprobates ; and though grace de-
posed sin in them from the throne, yet, O, what
offensive and God-provoking corruptions daily
break out in the best hearts ! Consider them in
their outward condition, and they are inferior, for
the most part, to others, 1 Cor. i. 26—28. " I
thank thee, O Father," saith Christ, " that thou
hast hid these things from the wise and prudent,
and hast revealed them unto babes," Matt. xi. 25.

And now let us consider and admire, that ever
this great and blessed God should be so much
concerned as you have heard he is, in all his providences, about such vile, despicable worms as we

are! He needs us not, but is perfectly blessed and happy in himself without us. We can add nothing to him. "Can a man be profitable to God?" Job xxii. 2. No; the holiest of men add nothing to him; yet see how great account he makes of us. For,

1. Doth not his eternal, electing love bespeak the dear account he made of us? Eph. i. 4, 5. How ancient, how free, and how astonishing is this act of grace! This is that design which all providences are in pursuit of, and will not rest till they have executed.

2. Doth not the gift of his only Son, out of his bosom, bespeak this truth, that God makes great account of this vile thing, man? Never was man so magnified before. If David could say, "When I consider thy heavens, the work of thy hands, the moon, and the stars, which thou hast ordained, Lord, what is man?" Psal. viii. 3, how much more may we say, when we consider thy Son, that lay in thy bosom, his infinite excellency, and unspeakable dearness to thee; Lord, what is man, that such a Christ should be delivered to death for him? for him, and not for fallen angels? Heb. ii. 16; for him, when in a state of enmity with God? Rom. v. 8.

3. Doth not the assiduity of His providential care for us speak his esteem of us? "Lest any hurt it, I will keep it night and day," Isa. xxvii. 3. "He withdraweth not his eyes from the righteous," Job xxxvi. 7. No, not for a moment all their days; for, did he so, a thousand mischiefs, in that moment, would rush in upon them, and ruin them.

4. Doth not the tenderness of his Providence speak his esteem for us? "As one whom his mo-

ther comforteth, so will I comfort you," Isa. lxvi.
13. He comforts his, by refreshing providences,
as an indulgent mother her tender child. So Isa.
xxxi. 5. As birds fly to their nests, when their
young are in danger, so he defends his. No tenderness in the creature can shadow forth the tender bowels of the Creator.

5. Doth not the variety of the fruits of his providence speak it? "Our mercies are new every
morning," Lam. iii. 23. See Psal. xl. 5. It is a
fountain from which do stream forth spiritual and
temporal, ordinary and extraordinary, public and
personal mercies, mercies without number.

6. Doth not the ministration of angels in the
providential kingdom speak it? "Are they not all
ministering spirits sent forth to minister," Heb.
i. 14.

Doth not the Providence which this day calls
us to celebrate the memory of, bespeak the great
account God hath for his people? O, if not so,
why had we not been given up as a prey to their
teeth? See Psal. cxxiv. If the Lord had not been
on our side, then wicked men, there compared to
fire, water, and wild beasts, had devoured us. O
blessed be God for that teeming providence which
hath already brought forth more than seventy
years' liberty and peace to the church of God. I
shall move in behalf of this providence, that you
would do by it as the Jews by their Purim, Esth.
ix. 27, 28, and the rather, because we seem now
to be as near danger by the same enemy as ever
since that time; and if such a mercy as this be
forgotten, God may say, "I will deliver you no
more," Judges x. 13.

Having proved the concerns of the people of
God to be conducted by the care of special Provi-

dence, and given various instances to show what
influence Providence hath upon those interests
and concerns of theirs among the rest; we come,
in the next place, to prove it to be the duty of the
people of God to reflect upon these performances
of Providence for them at all times, but especially
in times of strait and troubles.

This I will evidence to be your unquestionable
duty, by the following particulars:

1. This is our duty, because God hath expressly
commanded it, and called his people to make
the most serious reflections upon his works whether
of mercy or judgment. So, when that most
dreadful of all judgments was executed upon his
professing people, for their apostasy from God,
and God had removed the symbols of his presence
from among them, the rest are bid to go, that
is, by their meditations, (to send at least their
thoughts,) to Shiloh, and "see what God did to
it," Jer. vii. 12. So for mercies, God calls us to
consider and review them. "Remember, O my
people, from Shittim unto Gilgal, that ye may
know the faithfulness of the Lord," Mic. vi. 5, as
if he had said, If you reflect not upon that signal
providence, my faithfulness will be covered, and
your unfaithfulness discovered. So, for God's
works of providence about the creatures, we are
called to consider them, that we may prop up our
faith by those considerations, for our own supplies; "consider the fowls and the lilies," Matt.
vi. 26, 28.

2. It is plain that this is our duty, because the
neglect of it is every where in Scripture condemned as a sin. To be of a heedless, unobservant
temper, is very displeasing to God; and so much
appears from this Scripture, "Lord, when thy
10*

hand is lifted up they will not see," Isa. xxvi. 11.
Nay, it is a sin which God threatens and de-
nounces woe against in his word, Psal. xxviii. 4,
5, and Isa. v. 12, 13, yea, God not only threatens,
but smites men with visible judgments for this sin,
Job xxxiv. 26, 27.

3. For this end and purpose it is that the Holy
Ghost hath affixed those notes of attention to the
narrative of the works of Providence, in Scripture,
all which invite and call men to a due and clear
observation of them. So in that great and celebrated work of Providence, in delivering Israel out
of Egyptian bondage, you find a note of attention
twice affixed to it, Exod. iii. 2, 9. So, when that
daring enemy Rabshakeh, who put Hezekiah and
all the people into such a consternation, was de-
feated by Providence, there is a note of attention
prefixed to that providence : "Behold, I will send
a blast upon him," &c. 2 Kings xix. 7. So when
God glorifies his wisdom and power, in delivering
his people from their enemies, and ensnaring them
in the works of their own hands, a double note of
attention is affixed to that double work of Providence, "Higgaion; Selah," Psal. ix. 16. So, at
the opening of every seal, which contains a remarkable series or branch of Providence, how particularly is attention commanded to every one of
them ! "Come and see, come and see," Rev. vi.
1—7, &c. All these are very useless and super-
fluous additions in Scripture, if no such duty lies
upon us. See Psal. lxvi. 5.

4. Without due observation of the work of Providence, no praise can be rendered to God for any
of them. Praise and thanksgiving for mercies depend upon this act of observation of them, and cannot be performed without it. Psalm cvii. is spent

in narratives of God's providential care of men:
to his people in straits, ver. 4—6, to prisoners in
their bonds, ver. 10—12, to men that lie languishing in beds of sickness, ver. 17—19, to seamen
upon the stormy ocean, ver. 23, &c. to men in
times of famine, ver. 33—38, yea, his Providence
is displayed in all those changes that fall out in
the world, debasing the high and exalting the low,
ver. 40, 41, and, at every paragraph, men are still
called upon to praise God for each of these providences; but ver. 43, shows you what a necessary
ingredient to that duty observation is: "Whoso
is wise, and will observe those things, even they
shall understand the loving-kindness of the Lord;"
so that, of necessity, God must be defrauded of
his praise, if this duty be neglected.

5. Without this, we lose the usefulness and
benefit of all the works of God for us or others,
which would be an unspeakable loss indeed to us.
This is the food our faith lives upon in days of
distress. "Thou brakest the heads of leviathan
in pieces, and gavest him to be meat to the people
inhabiting the wilderness," Psal. lxxiv. 14, that is,
food to their faith. From providences past, saints
used to argue for fresh and new ones to come.
So David expresses himself: "The Lord that delivered me out of the paw of the lion, and out of
the paw of the bear, he will deliver me out of the
hand of this Philistine," 1 Sam. xvii. 37.   So
Paul, "Who hath delivered, and in whom also
we trust that he will yet deliver," 2 Cor. i. 10.
If these be forgotten, or not considered, the hands
of faith hang down.   "How is it that ye do not
remember, neither consider?" Matt. xvi. 9.   This
is a topic from which the saints had used to draw

their arguments in prayer for new mercies. As Moses, when he prays for continued or new pardons for the people, argues from what was past, " as thou hast forgiven them from Egypt until now," Numb. xiv. 19, so the church argues for new providences upon the same ground as Moses pleaded for new pardons, Isa. li. 9, 10.

6. It is a vile slighting of God not to observe what of himself he manifests in his providences; for, in all providences, especially in some, he comes nigh to us. He doth so in his judgments: " I will come nigh to you in judgment," Mal. iii. 5. He comes nigh in mercies also : "The Lord is nigh unto all them that call upon him," &c. Psal. cxlv. 18, yea, he is said to visit us by his providence when he corrects, Hos. ix. 7, and when he saves and delivers, Psal. cvi. 4. These visitations of God preserve our spirits, Job x. 12, and it is a wonderful condescension in the great God to visit us so often, " every morning and every moment," Job vii. 18. But not to take notice of it, is a vile and brutish contempt of God, Isa. i. 3, and Zeph. iii. 2. You would not do so by a man for whom you have any respect. It is the character of the wicked not to regard God's favours, Isa. xxvi. 10, or frowns, Jer. v. 3.

7. In a word, men can never order their addresses to God in prayer, suitably to their conditions, without due observation of his providences. Your prayers are to be suitable to your conditions; sometimes we are called to praise, sometimes to humiliation. In the way of his judgments you are to wait for him, Isa. xxvi. 8, to prepare to meet him, Zeph. ii. 1, 2. Amos iv. 12. Now your business is to turn away his anger, which you see

approaching; and sometimes you are called to
praise him for mercies received, Isa. xii. 1, 2, but
then you must observe them.

Thus you find the matter of David's psalms still
varied according to the providences that befell him;
but an inobservant, heedless spirit can never do it.
And thus you have the grounds of the duty briefly
represented.

Let us next, according to our method proposed,
proceed to show in what manner we are to reflect
upon the performances of Providence for us.   And
certainly it is not every slight and transient glance,
nor every cold, historical, unaffecting rehearsal, or
recognition, of his providences towards you, that
will pass with God for a discharge of this great
duty.   No: it is another manner of business than
the most of men understand it to be.   O that we
were but acquainted with this heavenly, spiritual
exercise! how sweet would it make our lives!
how light would it make our burdens!   Ah! sirs,
you live estranged from the pleasure of the Christian life while you live in the ignorance or neglect
of this duty.   Now, to lead you up to this heavenly, sweet, and profitable exercise, I will beg
your attention to the following directions :

First direction. Labour to get as full and thorough recognitions of the providences of God about
you, from first to last, as you are able.   O fill
your hearts with the thought of him and his
ways! If a single act of Providence be so ravishing and transporting, what would many such be,
if they were presented together to the view of the
soul ?   If one star be so beautiful to behold, what
is a constellation?   Let your reflections, therefore,
upon the acts and workings of Providence for you
be full, extensively and intensively.

1. Let them be as extensively full as may be. Search backward into all the performances of Providence throughout your lives, for so did Asaph; "I will remember the works of the Lord: surely I will remember thy wonders of old ; I will meditate of all thy work, and talk of thy doings," Psal. lxxvii. 11, 12. He laboured to recover and revive the ancient providences of God's mercies many years past, and sucked a fresh sweetness out of them by new reviews of them. Ah! sirs, let me tell you, there is not such a pleasant history for you to read in all the world, as the history of your own lives, if you would but sit down and record to yourselves, from the beginning hitherto, what God hath been to you, and done for you; what signal manifestations and out-breakings of his mercy, faithfulness, and love, there have been in all the conditions you have passed through ; if your hearts do not melt before you have gone half through that history, they are hard hearts indeed. "My Father, the guide of my youth."

2. Let them be as intensely full as may be. Let not your thoughts swim like feathers upon the surface of the waters, but sink like lead to the bottom. "The works of the Lord are great, sought out of them that have pleasure therein," Psal. cxi. 2. Not that I think it feasible to sound the depth of Providence by our short line, for "Thy way is in the sea, and thy path in the great waters, and thy footsteps are not known," Psal. lxxvii. 19, but it is our duty to dive as far as we can, and to admire the depth, when we cannot touch the bottom. It is in viewing providences, as it was with Elijah's servant, when he looked out for rain, 1 Kings xviii. 44, he went out once, and viewed the heavens, and saw nothing; but the

THE MYSTERY OF PROVIDENCE.   119

prophet bids him go again, and again, and look
upon the face of heaven seven times; and when he
had done so, What now? saith the prophet. "O
now," saith he, "I see a cloud rising like a man's
hand;" and then, keeping his eye upon it intent,
he sees the whole face of heaven covered with
clouds. So you may look upon some providences
once and again, and see little or nothing in them;
but look seven times, that is, meditate often upon
them, and you shall see their increasing glory like
that increasing cloud.

There are divers things to be distinctly pondered
and valued in one single providence, before you
can judge the amount and worth of it. The seasonableness of mercy may give it a very great
value; when it shall be timed so opportunely, and
fall out so seasonably, as may make it a thousand-
fold more considerable to you than the same mercy
would have been at another time. Thus, when
our wants are suffered to grow to an extremity,
and all visible hopes fail, then to have relief given
in, wonderfully enhances the price of such a mercy,
Isa. xli. 17, 18.

The peculiar care and kindness of Providence
to us, is a consideration which exceedingly height-
ens the mercy in itself, and endears it to us. So
when, in general calamities upon the world, we
are exempted, by the favour of Providence, covered
under its wings; when God shall call to us in evil
days, "Come, my people, enter thou into thy
chamber," Isa. xxvi. 19, 20, when such promises
shall be fulfilled to us in times of want and famine,
as in Psal. xxxiii. 18, 19, when others are aban-
doned and exposed to misery, who have every way
as much, it may be much more visible security
against it, and yet they delivered up, and we saved:

O, how endearing are such providences! Psal.
xci. 7, 8.

The introductiveness of a providence is of special regard and consideration, and by no means to
be neglected by us. There are leading providences
which, how slight and trivial they may seem in
themselves, yet, in this respect, justly challenge
the first rank among providential favours to us, because they usher in a multitude of other mercies,
and draw a blessed train of happy consequences
after them. Such a providence was that of Jes-
se's sending David with provisions to his brethren
that lay encamped in the army, 1 Sam. xvii. 17.
And thus every Christian may furnish himself out
of his own stock of experience, if he will but reflect and consider the place where he is, the relations that he hath, and the way by which he was
led into them.

The instruments employed by Providence for
you are of a special consideration ; and the finger
of God is clearly seen by us when we pursue that
meditation: for sometimes great mercies shall be
conveyed to us by very improbable means, and
more probable ones laid aside. A stranger shall
be stirred up to do that for you which your near
relations in nature had no power or will to do for
you. Jonathan, a mere stranger to David, cleaved
closer to him, and was more friendly and useful to
him, than his own brethren, who despised and
slighted him. Ministers have found more kindness and respect from strangers, than their own
people, who are more obliged to them. " A prophet," saith Christ, " is not without honour, save
in his own country, among his own kin, and in
his own house," Mark vi. 4.

Sometimes by the hands of enemies as well as

strangers. "The earth helped the woman," Rev. xii. 16. God hath bowed the hearts of many wicked men to show great kindness to his people, Acts xxviii. 2.

Sometimes God makes use of instruments for good to his people, who designed nothing but evil and mischief to them. Thus Joseph's brethren were instrumental to his advancement in that very thing wherein they designed his ruin, Gen. l. 20.

The design and scope of Providence, what the aim and level of Providence is, must not escape our thorough consideration. And truly this, of all others, is the most warming and melting consideration. You have the general account of the aim of all providences in this Scripture: "And we know that all things work together for good to them that love God," Rom. viii. 28. A thousand friendly hands are at work for them to promote and bring about their happiness. O! this is enough to sweeten the bitterness of Providence to us, that we know it shall turn to our salvation! Phil. i. 19.

The respect and relation Providence bears to our prayers is of singular consideration, and a most taking and sweet meditation. Prayer honours Providence and Providence honours prayer. Great notice is taken of this in Scripture, Gen. xxiv. 45; Dan. ix. 20; Acts xii. 12. You have had the very petitions you asked of him. Providences have borne the very signatures of your prayers upon them. O how affectingly sweet are such mercies!

Second direction. In all your observation of Providence, have special respect to that word of God, which is fulfilled and made good to you thereby.

11

This is a clear truth, that all providences have
relation to the written word. Thus Solomon, in
his prayer, acknowledges that the promises and
providences of God went along, step by step, with
his father David, all his days; and that his hand
(put there for his providence) had fulfilled whatever
his mouth had spoken, 1 Kings viii. 24. So Joshua,
in like manner, acknowledges, that " not one thing
had failed of all the good things which the Lord
had spoken," Jos. xxiii. 14. He had carefully observed what relation the works of God had to his
word. He compared them together, and found an
exact harmony; and so may you too, if you will
compare them as he did.

This I shall the more insist upon, because it is
by some interpreters supposed to be the very scope
of the text. For, as was noted in the explication,
they supply and fill the sense with the things which
he hath promised; and so read the text thus: " I
will cry unto God most high, to God who performeth the things that he hath promised for me."

Now, though I see no reason to limit the sense
so narrowly, yet it cannot be denied that this is a
special part of its meaning. Let us, therefore, in
all our reviews of Providence, consider what word
of God, whether it be of threatening, caution, counsel, or promise, is at any time made good to us by
his providences. And hereby a two-fold excellent
advantage will result to us. 1. This will greatly
confirm to us the truth of the Scripture, when we
shall see its truth so manifest in the events. Certainly, had Scripture no other seal or attestation,
this alone would be an unanswerable argument of
its divinity. When men shall find, in all ages,
the work of God wrought so exactly according to
this model, that we may say, as we have read, or

heard, so have we seen; O how great a confirmation is here before our eyes! 2. This will abundantly direct and instruct us in our present duties,
under all providences.   We shall know hereby
what we have to do, and how to carry ourselves
under all changes of conditions.   You can learn
the voice and errand of the rod only from the word,
Psal. xciv. 12.   The word interprets the works
of God.   Providences in themselves are not a perfect guide; they often puzzle and entangle our
thoughts; but bring them to the word, and your
duty will be quickly manifested, "until I went
into the sanctuary, then I understood their end,"
Psal. lxxiii. 16, 17, and, not only their end, but
his own duty, to be quiet in an afflicted condition,
and not envy their prosperity.

Well, then, bring those providences you have
past through, or are now under, to the word, and
you will find yourselves surrounded with a marvellous light, and see the verification of the Scriptures in them.   I shall, therefore, here appeal to
your consciences, whether you have not found
these events of Providence falling out agreeable in
all respects with the word.

1. The word tells you, that it is your wisdom
and interest to keep close to its rules, and the duties
it prescribes, that the way of holiness and obedience is the wisest way: "This is your wisdom,"
Deut. iv. 5, 6.

Now, let the events of Providence speak whether
this be true or not.   Certainly it will appear to be
so, whether we respect our present comfort, or
future happiness, both which we may see daily
exposed by departure from duty, and secured by
keeping close to it.   Let the question be asked of
the drunkard, adulterer, or profane swearer, when,

by sin, they have ruined body, soul, estate, and
name, whether it be their wisdom to walk in those
forbidden paths, after their own lusts; whether
they had not better consult their own interests and
comfort in keeping within the bounds and limits of
God's commands; and they cannot but confess,
that this their way is their folly. "What fruit,"
saith the apostle, "had ye in those things whereof
ye are now ashamed? for the end of those things
is death," Rom. vi. 21. Doth not the providence
of God verify upon them those threatenings which
are written in the experience of all ages? Prov.
xxiii. 21, 29, 30; Prov. v. 9; Job xxxi. 12; all
which woes and miseries they escape that walk
in God's statutes. Look upon all the ruined estates
and bodies you may every where see, and behold
the truth of the Scriptures evidently made good in
those sad providences.

2. The word tells you, that your departure from
the way of integrity and simplicity, to make use of
sinful policies, shall never profit you, 1 Sam. xii.
21; Prov. iii. 5.

Let the events of Providence speak to this also;
ask your own experience, and you shall have a full
confirmation of this truth. Did you ever leave the
way of simplicity and integrity, and use sinful
shifts to bring about your own designs, and prosper in that way? Certainly God hath cursed all
the ways of sin? and whoever finds them to thrive
with them, his people shall not. Israel would not
rely upon the Lord, but trust in the shadow of
Egypt; and what advantage had they by this sinful policy? See Isa. xxx. 1—5. David used a
great deal of sinful policy to cover his wicked
deed; but did it prosper? See 2 Sam. xii. 12. Sinful policies, in their first appearances, are pleasant

THE MYSTERY OF PROVIDENCE.   125

and promising; in their management, difficult; in
their event, sad.   Some, by sinful ways, have got-
ten wealth: but that Scripture hath been verified in
their experience, "Treasures of wickedness profit
nothing," Prov. x. 2.   Either God hath blown
upon it by a secret curse, that it hath done them
no good, or given them such disquietness in their
consciences that they have been forced to vomit it
up ere they could find peace, Job xi. 13—15.

That which David gave in charge to Solomon
hath been found experimentally true by thousands,
1 Chron. xxii. 12, 13; that the true way to prosperity is to keep close to the rule of the word! and
that the true reason why men cannot prosper, is
their forsaking that rule, 2 Chron. xxiv. 20.

It is true, if God have a purpose to destroy a
man, he may for a time suffer him to succeed and
prosper in his sin for his greater hardening, Job
xii. 6.   But it is not so with those whom the Lord
loves; their sinful shifts shall never thrive with
them.

3. The word prohibits your trust and confidence
in the creature, even in the greatest and most powerful among creatures, Psal. cxlvi. 3; it tells us that
it is better to trust in the Lord, than in them, Psal.
cxviii. 9.   It forbids our confidence in those creatures that are most nearly allied and related in the
bonds of nature to us, Mic. vii. 5.   It curseth the
man that gives that reliance to the creature which
is due to God, Jer. xvii. 5.

Consult the events of Providence in this case,
and see whether the word be not verified therein.
Did you ever lean upon an Egyptian reed, and did
it not break under you, and pierce as well as deceive you?   O, how often hath this been evident
in our experience!   Whatsoever we have over-

loved, idolized, and leaned upon, God hath, from time to time, broken it, and made us to see the vanity of it; so that we find the readiest course to be rid of our comforts is to set our hearts inordinately or immoderately upon them; for our God is a jealous God, and will not part with his glory to another. The world is full of examples of persons deprived of their comforts, husbands, wives, children, estates, &c., upon this account and by this means. If Jonah be overjoyed in his gourd, a worm is presently prepared to smite it. Hence it is that so many graves are opened for the burying of our idols out of our sight. If David say, " My mountain shall stand strong, I shall not be moved ;" the next news he shall hear, is of darkness and trouble, Psal. xxx. 6, 7. O how true and faithful do we find these sayings of God to be! Who cannot put to his seal, and say, Thy words are truth ?

4. The word assures us, that sin is the cause and inlet of affliction and sorrow, and that there is an inseparable connexion between them : " Be sure your sin will find you out," Num. xxxii. 23, that is, the sad effects and afflictions that follow it shall find you out. " If his sons forsake my law, I will visit their iniquities with rods," Psal. lxxxix. 30—32.

Inquire now at the mouth of Providence whether this be indeed so, according to the reports of the word. Ask but your own experiences, and you shall find, that just so Providence hath ordered it all along your way. When did you grow into a secure, vain, carnal frame, but you found some rousing, startling providence sent to awaken you? When did you wound your consciences with guilt, and God did not wound you for it in some other of your beloved enjoyments? Nay, so ordinary is this with God, that, from the observations of their own frames and ways, many Christians have fore-boded and presaged troubles at hand.

I do not say that God never afflicts his people but for their sin; for he may do it for their trial, 1 Pet. iv. 12; nor do I say that God follows every sin with a rod; for who then should stand before him? Psal. cxxx. 3, but this I say, that it is God's usual way to visit the sins of his people with rods of affliction, and this is in mercy to their souls. Upon this account it was, that the rod of God was upon David in a long succession of troubles upon his kingdom and family, after that great prevarica-tion of his, 2 Sam. xii. 9, 10. And if we would carefully search out the seeds and principles of those miseries, under which we or ours do groan, we should find them to be our own turnings aside from the Lord, according to Jer. ii. 19—iv. 18. Have not all these cautions and threatenings of the word been exactly fulfilled by Providence in your own experience? Who can but see the infallible truth of God in all that he hath threatened? And no less evident is the truth of the promises to all that will observe how Providence makes them good every day to us; for, consider,

5. What great security God hath given to his people, in the promises, that no man shall lose any thing by self-denial, for his sake. He hath told us, " Verily, I say unto you, there is no man that hath left house, or brethren, or sisters, or father, or mother, or wife, or children, or lands, for my sake and the gospel's; but he shall receive a hundred fold in this time, houses, and brethren, and sisters, and mothers, and children, and lands with perse-

cutions, and, in the world to come, eternal life,"
Mark x. 29, 30.

Though that vile apostate, Julian, derided this
promise, yet thousands and tens of thousands have
experienced it, and do at this day stand ready to
set their seal to it. God hath made it good to his
people, not only in spirituals, inward joy, and peace,
but even in temporals also. Instead of natural relations who took care for them before, hundreds of
Christians shall stand ready to assist and help
them; so that, though they have left all for Christ,
yet they may say with the apostle, " as having nothing, and yet possessing all things," 2 Cor. vi. 10.
O the admirable care and tenderness of Providence
over those that, for conscience sake, have left all
and cast themselves upon its immediate care! Are
there not, at this day, to be found many so provided for, even to the envy of their enemies, and
their own admiration? Who sees not the faithfulness of God in the promises, that hath but a heart
to trust God in them?

6. The word of promise assures us, that whatever wants and straits the saints fall into, their God
" will never leave them nor forsake them," Heb.
xiii. 5, that " he will be with them in trouble,"
Psal. xci. 15.

Consult the various providences of your life to
this point, and I doubt not but you will find the
truth of these promises as often confirmed as you
have been in trouble. Ask your own hearts, where
or when was it that your God forsook you, and
left you to sink and perish under your burden? I
doubt not, but most of you have been at one time
or other plunged in difficulties, difficulties out of
which you could see no way of escape by the eye

of reason ; yea such as, it may be, staggered your
faith in the promise, as David's was, when he said,
" I shall one day perish by the hand of Saul,"
1 Sam. xxvii. 1. " All men are liars," even
Samuel himself; and yet, notwithstanding all, we
see him emerge out of that sea of trouble, and the
promises made good in every tittle to him. You
may, doubtless, observe the like in your own cases.
Ask your own souls the question, and they will
satisfy it. Did God abandon and cast you off in
the day of your straits? Certainly you must belie
your own experience, if you should say so. It is
true, there have been some plunges and difficulties
you have met with, wherein you could see no way
of escape, but concluded you must perish in them;
difficulties that have staggered your faith in the
promises, and made you doubt whether the Fountain of all-sufficiency would let out itself for your
relief; yea, such difficulties as have tempted you
to murmuring and impatience, and thereby provoked the Lord to forsake you in your straits ; but
yet you see he did not. He hath either strengthened your back to bear, or lightened your burden,
or opened an unexpected door of escape, according
to that promise, 1 Cor. x. 13, so that the evil
which you feared came not upon you.

7. You read, that the word of God is the only
support and relief to a gracious soul in the dark
day of affliction, Psal. cxix. 50, 92 ; 2 Sam. xxiii.
5; that for this very purpose it was written,
Rom. xv. 4. No rules of moral prudence, no sensual remedies, can perform that for us which the
word can do.

And is not this a sealed truth, attested by a thousand undeniable experiences? Hence have the
saints fetched their cordials when fainting under

the rod. One word of God can do more than ten
thousand words of men to relieve a distressed soul.
If Providence have at any time directed you to
such promises as either assure you that the Lord
will be with you in trouble, Psal. xci. 15, or, that
encourage you from inward peace, to bear cheerfully outward burdens, John xvi. 33, or satisfy you
of God's tenderness and moderation in his dealings
with you, Isa. xxvii. 8, or that you shall reap
blessed fruits from them, Rom. viii. 28, or that
clear up your interest in God, and his love under
your afflictions, 2 Sam. vii. 14; O! what sensible
ease and relief ensues! How light is your burden
compared with what it was before!

8. The word tells us, that there is no such way
to improve our estates, as to lay them out with a
cheerful liberality for God: and that our withholding our hands, when God and duty calls to distri-
bute, will not be for our advantage. See Prov. xi.
24, 25; Isa. xxxii. 8; Prov. xix. 17.

Consult Providence now, and you shall find it,
in all respects, according to the report of the word.
O how true is the Scripture testimony herein!
There are many thousand witnesses now living,
who can set their seals to both parts of this propo-
sition. What men save (as they count saving)
with one hand, Providence scatters by another
hand; and what they scatter abroad with a liberal
hand and single eye for God, is surely repaid to
them or theirs. Never did any man lose by dis-
tributing for God. He that lends to the poor, puts
his money to interest to the Lord, as some expound
that text. Some have observed, how Providence
hath doubled all they have laid out for God in ways
unexpected to them.

9. The word assures us, that the best expedient

for a man to settle his own interest, in the consciences and affections of men, is to direct his ways so as to please the Lord, Prov. xvi. 7, and doth not Providence confirm it? This the three Jews found by experience, Dan. iii. 28, 29, and so did Daniel, vi. 20—22. This kept up John's reputation in the conscience of Herod, Mark vi. 20. So it fell out when Constantius made that exploratory decree; those who were conscientious were preferred, and those who changed their religion, were expelled. Never did any man lose at last by his fidelity.

10. The written word tells us that the best expedient to inward peace and tranquillity of mind, under puzzling and distracting troubles, is to commit ourselves and our case to the Lord; so you read, Psalm xxxvii. 5—7, and Prov. xvi. 3.

And as you have read in the word, so you have found it in your own experience. O! what a burden is off your shoulders, when you have resigned the case to God! Then doth Providence issue your affairs comfortably for you. The difficulty is soon over, when the heart is brought to this.

Thus you see how Scriptures are fulfilled by Providence in these few instances I have given of it. Compare them in all other cases, and you shall find the same; for all the lines of Providence lead from the Scriptures, and return thither again, and do most visibly begin and end there.

Third direction. In all your reviews and observations of Providence, be sure that you eye God as the author and orderer of them all, Prov. iii. 6.

1. In all the comfortable providences of your lives eye God as the author or donor of them. Remember he is the Father of mercies, that begets every mercy for you: " The God of all comfort,"

2 Cor. i. 3, without whose order no mercy or comfort can come to your hands. And think it not enough thus to acknowledge him in a general way; but, when you receive mercies, take special notice of the following particulars:

(1.) Eye the care of God for you, 1 Pet. v. 7. He careth for you; "your Father knows ye have need of these things," Matt. vi. 32. It is but to acquaint him what you want, and your wants are supplied, Phil. iv. 6. Torture not yourselves about it, you have a Father that cares for you.

(2.) Eye the wisdom of God in the way of dispensing his mercies to you, how suitably they are ordered to your condition, and how seasonably. When one comfort is cut off, and removed, another is raised up in its room. Thus Isaac was comforted in Rebecca after his mother's death, Gen. xxiv. 67.

(3.) Eye the free grace of God in them, yea see riches of grace in every bequest of comfort to such vile and unworthy creatures as you are. See yourselves over-topped by the least of all your mercies; "I am not worthy of the least," said Jacob, Gen. xxxii. 10.

(4.) Eye the condescension of God to your requests for those mercies, Psal. xxxiv. 6. This is the sweetest bit in any enjoyment, in which a man can sensibly relish the return and answer of his prayers, and greatly inflames the soul's love te God, Psal. cxvi. 1.

(5.) Eye the design and end of God, in all your comforts. Know that it is not sent to satisfy the cravings of your sensual appetite, but to quicken and enable you for a more cheerful discharge of your duty, Deut. xxviii. 47.

(6.) Eye the way and method in which your

mercies are conveyed to you. They all flow to you through the blood of Christ, and covenant of grace, 1 Cor. iii. 22, 23. Mercies derive their sweetness from the channel through which they run to us.

(7.) Eye the distinguishing goodness of God in all the comfortable enjoyments of your lives. How many thousands, better than you, are denied those comforts ! See Heb. xi. 37.

(8.) Eye them all as comforts, appointed to refresh you in your way to far better and greater mercies than themselves. The best mercies are still reserved to the last, and all these are introductive of better.

2. In all the sad and afflictive providences that befall you, eye God as the author and orderer of them also ; so he represents himself to us ; " Behold, I frame evil against you, and devise a device against you," Jer. xviii. 11 ; and " Is there evil in the city, and the Lord has not done it ?" Amos iii. 6. More particularly,

(1.) Set before you the sovereignty of God. Eye him as a being infinitely superior to you, at whose pleasure, you, and all you have, are, Psal. cxv. 3, which is the most conclusive reason and argument of submission, Psal. xlvi. 10, for if we, and all we have, proceeded from his will, how equal is it that we be resigned up to it ? It is not many years ago since we were not, and, when it pleased him to bring us upon the stage of action, we had no liberty of contracting with him on what terms we would come into the world ; or, refuse to be, except we might have our being on such terms as we desired. His sovereignty is gloriously displayed in his eternal decrees and temporal providences. He might have put you into what

12

rank of creatures he pleased. He might have
made you the most despicable creatures, worms,
or toads ; or, if men, the most vile, abject, and
miserable ; and when you had run through all the
miseries of this life, have damned you to eternity,
made you miserable for ever, and all this without
any wrong to you. And shall not this quiet us
under the common afflictions of this life?

(2.) Set the grace and goodness of God before
you in all afflictive providences. O see him passing by you in the cloudy and dark day, proclaiming
his name, "The Lord, the Lord God, merciful and
gracious." There are two sorts of mercies that
are seldom eclipsed by the darkest affliction, which
befall the saints in their temporal concerns, namely, sparing mercy in this world, and saving mercy
in that to come. It is not so bad now as it might,
and we deserved it should be, and it will be better
hereafter. This the church observed, and reason-
ed herself quiet from it, Lam. iii. 22. Hath he
taken some? he might have taken all. Are we
afflicted? It is a mercy we are not destroyed.
O! if we consider what temporal mercies are yet
spared, and what spiritual mercies are bestowed,
and yet continued to us, we shall find cause to
admire mercy, rather than complain of severity.

(3.) Eye the wisdom of God in all your afflictions : behold it in the choice of the kind of your
affliction, this, and not another; the time, now, and
not at another season ; the degree, in this measure
only, and not in a greater; the supports afforded
you under it, not left altogether helpless; the issue,
to which it is overruled, it is to your good, not
ruin. Look upon all these, and then ask thy heart
that question God asked Jonah, "Dost thou well
to be angry?" Surely, when you consider all,

what need you have had of these rods, that your corruptions will require all this, it may be much more, to mortify them; that without the perishing of these things, you might have perished for ever; you will see great reason to be quiet and well satisfied under the hand of God.

(4.) Set the faithfulness of the Lord before you under the saddest providences. So did David, Psal. cxix. 75. This is according to his covenant faithfulness, Psal. lxxxix. 32. Hence it is, that the Lord will not withhold a rod when need requires it, 1 Pet. i. 6, nor will he forsake his people under the rod, when he inflicts it, 2 Cor. iv. 9.

O! what quietness will this breed! I see my God will not lose my heart, if a rod can prevent it; he had rather hear me groan here, than howl hereafter; his love is judicious, not fond; he consults my good, rather than my ease.

(5.) Eye the all-sufficiency of God in the day of affliction. See enough in him still, whatever be gone. Here is the fountain still as full as ever, though this or that pipe be cut off, which was wont to convey somewhat of it to me. O Christians, cannot you make up any loss this way? Cannot you see more in God than in any, or all the creature-comforts you have lost? With what eyes, then, do you look upon God?

(6.) Eye the immutability of God. Look on him as the Rock of ages, "the Father of lights, with whom is no variableness, nor shadow of turning," James i. 17. Eye Jesus Christ as "the same yesterday, to-day, and for ever." O, how quietly will you then behave yourselves under the changes of Providence! It may be, two or three days have made a sad change in your condition! the death of a dear relation hath turned all things upside down: that place is empty where lately he was, "his place shall know him no more," Job vii. 10. Well, but God is what he was, and where he was; time shall make no change upon him; "the grass withereth, the flower fadeth, but the word of the Lord abideth for ever," Isa. xl. 8. O! how composing are those views of God to our spirits, under dark providences!

Fourth direction. Work up your hearts to those frames, and exercise those affections which the several providences of God, that are about you, call for, Eccles. vii. 14. Suit yourselves to answer the design and end of God in all providences. As there are various affections planted in your souls, so are there several graces planted in those affections, and several providences appointed to draw forth and exercise these graces.

When the providences of God are sad and afflictive, either upon the church in general, or your families and persons in particular, then it is seasonable for you to exercise godly sorrow, and humility of spirit; for in that day, and by those providences, God doth call to it, Isa. xxii. 12; Micah vi. 9. Now sensitive pleasure and natural joy is out of season; "should we then make mirth?" Ezek. xxi. 10. If there be either a filial spirit in us, we cannot be light and vain, when our Father is angry; or, if any real sense of the evil of sin, which provokes God's anger, we must be heavy-hearted when God is smiting for it; or, if any sense and compassion for the miseries that sin brings upon the world, it will make us say with David, "I beheld the transgressors, and was grieved," Psal. cxix. 158. It is sad to consider the miseries that they pull down upon themselves in this world, and that to come. If there be any care in us to prevent utter ruin, and stop God in the way of his anger, we know this is the means to do it, Amos iv. 12.

How sad and dismal soever the face of Providence be, yet still maintain spiritual joy and comfort in God under all. "Though there be no herd in the stall, yet will I rejoice in the Lord, I will joy in the God of my salvation," Hab. iii. 17, 18. There are two sorts of comforts—natural and sensitive, divine and spiritual. There is a time when it becomes Christians to exercise both; so Esth. ix. 22. And there is a time when the former is to be suspended, and laid by, Psal. cxxxvii. 2 But there is no season wherein spiritual joy and comfort in God is unseasonable, as appears by those Scriptures, 1 Thess. v. 16, and Phil. iv. 4. This spiritual joy, or comfort, is nothing else but the cheerfulness of our heart in God, and the sense of our interest in him and in his promises; and it is sure that no providence can render this unseasonable to a Christian. Let us suppose the most afflictive and calamitous state a Christian can be incident to; yet, why should sad providences make him lay by his comforts in God? Whereas those are but for a moment, but these eternal, 2 Cor. iv. 17.

Why should we lay by our joy in God upon the account of sad providences without, when, at the very worst and lowest ebb, the saints have infinitely more cause to rejoice, than to be cast down? There is more in one of their mercies to comfort them, than in all their troubles to deject them. All your losses are but as the loss of a farthing to a prince, Rom. viii. 18.

Why should they be sad as long as their God is with them in all their troubles? As Christ saith,

12*

"Can the children of the bride-chamber be sad,
whilst the bridegroom is with them? Matt. ix.
15. So say I: Can the soul be sad, whilst God
is with it? O! methinks that one promise, "I
will be with him in trouble," Psal. xci. 15, should
bear you up under all burdens. Let them be cast
down that have no God in trouble to turn to.

Why should they be sad as long as no outward
dispensation of Providence, be it ever so sad, can
be interpreted as a mark or sign of God's hatred,
or enmity? "There is one event to the righteous
and the wicked," Eccles. ix. 2, 3. Indeed, if it
were a signification of the Lord's wrath against a
man, it would justify our dejection; but this cannot be so; his heart is full of love, whilst the face
of Providence is full of frowns.

Why should we be cast down under sad providences, whilst we have such great security, that
even, by the hands of these providences, God will
do us good, and all these things shall "turn to our
salvation?" Rom. viii. 28. By these, God is but
killing your lusts, weaning your hearts from a vain
world, preventing temptations, and exciting desires after heaven; this is all the hurt they shall
do; and shall that sadden us?

Why should we lay by our joy in God when
the change of our condition is so nigh? It is but
a little while, and sorrows shall flee away; you
shall never suffer more: " God will wipe away all
tears," Rev. vii. 17. Well, then, you see there is
no reason, upon the account of Providence, to give
up your joy and comfort in God. But if you will
maintain it under all providences, then be careful

1. To clear up your interest in and title to God.
Faith may be separated from comfort, but assurance cannot.

2. Mortify your inordinate affections to earthly things. This makes providences, that deprive and cross us, so heavy. Mortify your opinion and affection, and you sensibly lighten your affliction. It is a strong affection that makes strong affliction.

3. Dwell much upon the meditation of the Lord's near approach, and then all these things will seem but trifles to you. "Let your moderation be known unto all men : the Lord is at hand."

Exercise heavenly-mindedness, and keep your hearts upon things eternal, under all the providences with which the Lord exercises you in this world, Gen. vi. 9. Noah walked with God, yet met with as sad providences, in his day, as any man that ever lived since his time. But, alas! we find most providences rather stop than step in our walk with God. If we be under comfortable providences, how sensual, wanton, and worldly do our hearts grow! and if sad providences befall us, how indolent or distracted are we! And this comes to pass, partly through the narrowness, but mostly through the deceitfulness of our spirits. Our hearts are narrow, and know not how to manage two businesses of such different natures, as earthly and heavenly matters are, without detriment to one. But, certainly, such a frame of spirit is attainable that will enable us to keep on in an even and steady course with God, whatever befall us. Others have attained it, and why not we? Prosperous providences are for the most part a dangerous state to the soul. The moon never suffers an eclipse but at full; yet Jehoshaphat's grace suffered no eclipse from the fulness of his outward condition, who "had riches in abundance, and his heart was lifted up in the way of God's commandments," 2 Chron. xvii. 5, 6.

David's life was full of cares, turmoils, and in-
cumbrances, as most men we read of; yet how
spiritual the temper of his heart was, that excellent book of Psalms, the most of which was composed amidst those distractions, will acquaint us.
The apostles were cast into as great necessities,
and suffered as hard things as ever men did; yet
how raised and heavenly their spirits were amidst
all, who sees not? And certainly, if it were not
possible to maintain heavenly-mindedness in such
a state and posture of affairs, God would never exercise any of his people with such providences:
he would never give you so much of the world to
lose your hearts in the love of it; or so little, to
distract you with the cares of it. If, therefore, we
were more deeply sanctified, and the tendencies of
our hearts heaven-ward more ardent and vigorous;
if we were more mortified to earthly things, and
could but keep our due distance from them; our
outward conditions would not, at this rate, draw
forth and exercise our inward corruptions, nor
would we hazard the loss of so sweet an enjoyment as our fellowship with God is, for the sake
of any concern our bodies have on earth.

Under all providences, maintain a contented
heart with what the Lord allots you, be it more or
less of the things of this world. This grace must
run parallel with all providences. "Learn how
to be full, and how to suffer want, and in every
state to be content," Phil. iv. 12.

In this duty, all men are concerned at all times,
and in every state, not only the people of God, but
even the unregenerate also. I will therefore address some considerations proper to both. And,
first, to the unregenerate, to stop their mouths from
repining, and charging God foolishly, when Pro-

vidence crosses them. Let them seriously consider these four things:

(1.) That hell and eternal damnation are the
portion of their cup, according to the tenor of the
law and gospel threatenings. Whatsoever, therefore, is short of this is to be admired as the fruit
of God's stupendous patience and forbearance towards them. Ah! poor souls! know you not that
you are men and women, condemned to wrath by
the plain sentence of the law! Mark xvi. 16. John
iii. 36. 2 Thess. i. 6, 7. And if so, surely there
are other matters to exercise your thoughts, desires,
fears, and care about, than these. Alas! if you
cannot bear a frown of providence, a light cross in
these things, how will you bear everlasting burn-
ings? A man that is to lose his head to-morrow,
is not very solicitous what bed he lies on, or how
his table is furnished the night before.

(2.) Consider, though you be condemned persons, and have no promise to entitle you to any
mercy, yet there are very many mercies in your
possession at this day. Be your condition as
afflictive as it will, is life nothing? especially considering, whither you must sink when that thread
is cut. Are the necessary supports of life nothing?
Doth not Providence minister to you these things,
though you daily disoblige it, and provoke God to
send you to your own place? But, above all, is
the gospel and precious means of salvation nothing,
by which you yet are in a capacity of escaping the
damnation of hell? O what would the damned say,
if they were but put into your condition once more?
What! and yet fret against God, because every
thing else suits not your desires?

(3.) Consider, that if ever you be rescued out
of that miserable condition you are in, such cross

providences as these you complain of are the most
probable means to do it. Alas! prosperity and
success is not the way to save, but destroy you,
Prov. i. 32. You must be bound in fetters, and
holden in cords of affliction, if ever your ear be
opened to instruction, Job xxxvi. 8—10. Woe to
you, if you go on smoothly in the way in which
you are, and meet with no crosses.

(4.) Consider all your troubles, under which
you complain, are pulled down upon your heads by
your own sins. You turn God's mercies into sin,
and then fret against God, because he turns your
sins into sorrow. Your ways and doings procure
these things to you. Lay your hand, therefore,
upon your mouth, and say, " Why doth a living
man complain, a man for the punishment of his
sin?" Lam. iii. 39. But I must turn to the Lord's
people, who have least pretences of all men to be
dissatisfied with any of God's providences, and
yet are but too frequently found in that temper.
And to them I shall offer the following considerations :

[1.] Consider your spiritual mercies and privileges with which the Lord Jesus hath invested you,
and repine at your lot of providence if you can.
One of these mercies alone hath enough in it to
sweeten all your troubles in this world. When
the apostle considered them, his heart was overwhelmed with astonishment, so that he could not
forbear, in the midst of all his outward troubles, to
cry out, " Blessed be the God and Father of our
Lord Jesus Christ, who hath blessed us with all
spiritual blessings," &c. Eph. i. 3. O! who that
sees such an inheritance settled upon him in Christ
can ever open his mouth more to repine at his lot
of providence?

[2.] Consider your sins, and that will make you contented with your lot. Yea, consider these two things in sin : what it deserves from God, and what it requires to mortify and purge it in you. It deserves from God eternal ruin; the merit of hell is in the least vain thought. Every sin forfeits all the mercies you have; and if so, rather wonder your mercies are so many, than that you have no more. Besides, you cannot doubt but your corruptions require all the crosses, wants, and troubles, that are upon you, and, it may be, a great deal more, to mortify and subdue them. Do not you find, after all the rods that have been upon you, a proud heart still, a vain and earthly heart still? O! how many bitter potions are necessary to purge out this tough, malignant humour!

[3.] Consider how near you are to the change of your condition. Have but a little patience, and all will be as well with you as your hearts can desire. It is no small comfort to the saints, that this world is the worst place that ever they shall be in; things will be better every day with them. If the traveller have spent all his money, yet it doth not much trouble him, if he know himself within a few miles of his own home. If there be no candles in the house, we do not much care for it, if we are sure it is almost break of day; for then there will be no use for them. This is your case: " Your salvation is nearer than when you believed," Rom. xiii. 12.

I have done with the directive part of this discourse; but before I proceed further, I judge it necessary to leave a few cautions to prevent the abuse of Providence, and your miscarriages in your behaviour towards it.

First caution. If Providence delay the perform-

ance of any mercy to you, that you have long
waited and prayed for, yet see that you despond not,
nor grow weary of waiting upon God for that reason. It pleases the Lord oftentimes to try and exercise his people this way, and make them cry,
" How long, Lord, how long?" Psal. xiii. 1, 2.

These delays, both upon spiritual and temporal
accounts, are frequent, and, when they befall us,
we are too apt to interpret them as denials, and
fall into a sinful despondency of mind, though there
be no cause at all for it, Psal. xxxi. 12, and Lam.
iii. 8, 44. It is not always that the returns of
prayer are despatched to us in the same hour they
are asked of God; yet sometimes it falls out so,
Isa. lxv. 24, and Dan. ix. 23. But though the
Lord means to perform to us the mercies we desire,
yet he will ordinarily exercise our patience to wait
for them ; and that for these reasons : 1. Because
our time is not the proper season for us to receive
our mercies in. Now the season of mercy is a
very great circumstance, that adds much to the
value of it. God judges not as we do ; we are all
in haste, and will have it now, " But he is a God
of judgment, and blessed are they that wait for
him," Isa. xxx. 18. 2. Afflictive providences have
not accomplished that design upon our hearts which
they were sent for, when we are so earnest and
impatient for a change of them, and till then the
rod must not be taken off, Isa. x. 12. 3. The more
prayers and searchings of heart come between our
wants and supplies, our afflictions and reliefs, the
sweeter are our reliefs and supplies thereby made
to us. " This is our God, we have waited for him,
and he will save us: this is the Lord, we have
waited for him, we will rejoice and be glad in his
salvation," Isa. xxv. 9. This recompenses the

delay, and pays us for all the expenses of our patience.

But though there be such weighty reasons for the stop and delay of refreshing, comfortable providences, yet we cannot bear it, our hands hang down, and we faint, " I am weary of my crying, my throat is dry, mine eyes fail, while I wait for my God," Psal. lxix. 3. For alas! we judge by sense and appearance, and consider not that God's heart may be towards us, whilst the hand of his Providence seems to be against us. If things continue at one rate with us, we think our prayers are lost, and our hopes perished from the Lord: much more when things grow worse and worse, and our darkness and trouble increase, as usually they do, just before the break of day and change of our condition; then we conclude God is angry with our prayers. See Gideon's reply, Judg. vi. 13. This even staggered the faith of a Moses, Exod. v. 22, 23. O what groundless jealousies and suspicions of God are found at such times in the hearts of his own children! Job ix. 16, 17, and Psal. lxxvii. 7—9.

But this is our great evil, and, to prevent it in future trials, I will offer a few proper considerations in the case:

1. The delay of your mercies is really for your advantage. You read, that the Lord waits that he may be gracious," Isa. xxx. 18. What is that? Why, it is nothing else but the time of his preparation of mercies for you and your hearts, for mercy that so ye may have it with the greatest advantage of comfort. The foolish child would pluck the apple whilst it is green; but, when it is ripe, it drops off of its own accord, and is more pleasant and wholesome.

2. It is a greater mercy to have a heart willing to refer all to God, and to be at his disposal, than to enjoy presently the mercy we are most eager and impatient for: in that, God pleases you; in this, you please God. A mercy may be given you as the fruit of common providence, but such a temper of heart is the fruit of special grace. So much as the glorifying of God is better than the content and pleasure of the creature, so much is such a frame better than such a fruition.

3. Expected mercies are never nearer than when the hearts and hopes of God's people are lowest. Thus in their deliverance out of Egypt and Baby-lon, Ezek. xxxvii. 11, so we have found it in our own personal concerns: "At evening time it shall be light," Zech. xiv. 7. When we look for in-creasing darkness, light arises.

4. Our unfitness for mercies is the reason why they are delayed so long. We put the blocks into the way of mercy, and then repine that they make no more haste to us. "The Lord's hand is not shortened, but our iniquities have separated between him and us," Isa. lix. 1, 2.

5. Consider, the mercies you wait for are the fruits of pure grace; you deserve them not, nor can claim them upon any title of desert; and there-fore have great reason to wait for them in a patient and thankful frame.

6. Consider how many millions of men, as good as you by nature, are cut off from all hope and ex-pectation of mercy for ever, and there remains to them nothing but "a fearful expectation of wrath." This might have been your case: and therefore be not of an impatient spirit, under the expectations of mercy.

Second caution.. Pry not too curiously into the

secrets of Providence, nor suffer your shallow reason arrogantly to judge and censure its designs.

There are hard texts in the works, as well as in the word of God. It becomes us modestly and humbly to reverence, but not to dogmatize too boldly and positively upon them ; a man may easily get a strain by over-reaching. " When I thought to know this," saith Asaph, " it was too wonderful for me." *I thought to know this:* there was the arrogant attempt of reason, there he pried into the arcana of Providence ; but *it was too wonderful for me:* it was but useless labour, as Calvin expounds it. He pried so far into that puzzling mystery of the afflictions of the righteous, and prosperity of the wicked, till it begat envy towards them, and despondency in himself, Psalm lxxiii. 3, 13, and this was all he got by summoning Providence to the bar of reason. Holy Job was guilty of this evil, and was ingenuously ashamed of it, Job xlii. 3.

I know there is nothing in the word, or in the works of God, that is repugnant to sound reason ; but there are some things in both, which are opposite to carnal reason, as well as above right reason ; and therefore our reason never shows itself more unreasonable, than in summoning those things to its bar, which transcend its sphere and capacity. Manifold are the mischiefs which ensue upon this practice. For, by this we are drawn into an unworthy suspicion and distrust of the faithfulness of God in the promises. Sarah laughed at the tidings of the son of promise, because reason contradicted and told her, it was naturally impossible, Gen. xviii. 13, 14. Hence come despondency of mind and faintness of heart, under afflictive providences, reason can discern no good fruits in them, nor de liverance from them, and so our hands hang down in a sinful discouragement, saying, "All these things are against us," Gen. xlii. 36. Hence flow temptations to deliver ourselves by indirect and sinful mediums, Isa. xxx. 15, 16. When our own reason fills us with a distrust of Providence, it naturally prompts us to sinful shifts, and there leaves us entangled in the snares of our own making.

Beware, therefore, you lean not too much to your own reason and understanding. Nothing is more plausible, nothing more dangerous. In other matters it is appointed the arbiter and judge: we make it so here; and, therefore, we are so diffident and distrustful, notwithstanding the fullest security of the promises, whilst our reason stands by unsatisfied.

Having given directions for the due management of this great and important duty, what remains, but that we now set our hearts to it, and make it the constant work of every day throughout our lives? O what peace, what pleasure, what stability, what holy courage and confidence would result from such an observation of Providence, as hath been directed to! But alas! we may say, with reference to the voices of Divine Providence, " God speaketh once, yea twice, yet man perceiveth it not," Job xxxiii. 14. Many a time Providence hath spoken instruction in duty, conviction for iniquity, encouragement under despondency; but we regard it not. How greatly are we all wanting to our duty and comfort by this neglect! It will be but needful therefore to spread before you the loveliness and excellency of walking with God in due and daily observation of his providences, that our souls may be fully engaged to it.

First motive. And first, let me offer this as a

moving argument to all gracious souls : That by this means you maintain sweet and sensible communion with God from day to day. And what is there desirable in this world in comparison therewith! "Thou, Lord, hast made me glad through thy work : I will triumph in the works of thy hands," Psal. xcii. 4 ; your hearts may be as sweetly and sensibly refreshed by the works of God's hands, as by the words of his mouth. Psalm civ. is spent in the consideration of the works of Providence, which so filled the Psalmist's heart, that, by way of ejaculation, he thus expresses the effect of it : "My meditation of him shall be sweet," ver. 34.

Communion with God, properly and strictly taken, consists in two things, namely, God's manifestation of himself to the soul, and the soul's answerable returns to God. This is that fellowship we have here with God. Now God manifests himself to his people by providences as well as ordinances ; neither is there any grace in a sanctified soul hid from the gracious influences of his providential manifestations. Sometimes the Lord manifests his displeasure and anger against the sins of his people in correcting and rebuking providences. His rods have a chiding voice : "Hear the rod, and who hath appointed it," Micah vi. 9. This discovery of God's anger kindly melts and thaws a gracious soul, and produces a double sweet effect upon it, namely, repentance for sins past, and due caution against future sins.

It thaws and melts the heart for sins committed. Thus David's heart was melted for his sin when the hand of God was heavy upon him in affliction, Psal. xxxii. 4, 5. Thus the captive church, upon whom fell the saddest and most dismal providence

13*

that ever befell any of God's people in any age of the world, see how their hearts are broken for sin under this severe rebuke, Lam. ii. 17—19. And then, in the next place, for caution against sin for the time to come. It is plain, that the rebukes of Providence leave that effect also upon gracious hearts, Ezra ix. 13, 14; Psal. lxxxv. 8.

Sometimes he cheers and comforts the hearts of his people with smiling and reviving providences, both public and personal. There are times of lifting up as well as casting down by the hand of Providence. The scene changes; the aspects of Providence are very cheerful and encouraging, their winter seems to be over; they put off their garments of mourning; and then, ah! what sweet returns are made to heaven by gracious souls! Doth God lift them up by prosperity? They will also lift up their God by praises. See Psal. xviii. 1—3. So Moses, and the people with him, Exod. xv., when God had delivered them from Pharaoh, how do they exalt him in a song of thanksgiving, which, for the elegance and spirituality of it, is made an emblem of the doxologies given to God in glory by the saints, Rev. xv. 3.

Upon the whole, whatever effects our communion with God, in any of his ordinances, doth use to produce upon our hearts, the same we may observe to follow our conversing with him, in his providences. For,

1. It is usually found, in the experience of all the saints, that, in what ordinance or duty soever they have any sensible communion with God, it naturally produces in their spirits a deep abasement and humiliation from the sense of divine condescensions to such vile, poor worms as we are. Thus Abraham, "I am but dust and ashes," Gen.

xviii. 27. The same effect follows our converse
with God in his providences. Thus when God
had, in the way of his providences, prospered
Jacob, how doth he lay himself at the feet of God,
as a man overwhelmed with the sense of mercy!
"And Jacob said, I am not worthy of the least of
all thy mercies, and of all the truth which thou
hast showed thy servant; for, with my staff I
passed over this Jordan, and now I am become
two bands," Gen. xxxii. 9, 10. Thus also it was
with David, "Who am I, and what is my father's
house, that thou hast brought me hitherto?" 2 Sam.
vii. 18. And I doubt not but some of you have
found the like frame of heart upon you that these
holy men here expressed. Can you not remember, when God lifted you up by providence, how
you cast down yourselves before him, and have
been viler in your own eyes than ever? Why,
thus do all gracious hearts: what am I that the
Lord should do thus and thus for me? O that ever
so great and holy a God should be thus concerned
for so vile and sinful a worm!

2. Doth communion with God in ordinances
melt the heart into love to God? Cant. ii. 3—5.
Why, so doth the observation of his providences
also. Never did any man converse with God's
works of providence aright, but found his heart, at
some times, melted into love to the God of his
mercies, Psal. xviii. 1, compared with the title.
When God had delivered him from the hand of
Saul, and all his enemies, he said, "I will love
thee, O Lord, my strength." Every man loves
the mercies of God, but a saint loves the God of
his mercies. The mercies of God, as they are the
fuel of a wicked man's lusts, so they are fuel to
maintain a good man's love to God; not that their

love to God is grounded upon these external benefits.   Not thine, but thee, O Lord! is the motto of
a gracious soul; but yet these things serve to blow
up the flame of love to God in their hearts, and
they find it so.

3. Doth communion with God set the keenest
edge upon the soul against sin?   You see it does,
and you have a striking instance of it in Moses,
when he had been with God in the mount for forty
days, and had there enjoyed communion with him!
when he came down and saw the calf the people
had made, see what a holy paroxysm of zeal and
anger it cast his soul into, Exod. xxxii. 19, 20.
Why, the same effect you may discern to follow
the saints' converse with God in his providences.
What was that which pierced the heart of David
with such a deep sense of the evil of his sin, which
was so abundantly manifested in Psal. li. throughout?   Why, if you look into the title you shall find
it was the effect of what Nathan had laid before
him: and if you consult 2 Sam. xii. 7—10, you
shall find it was the goodness of God manifested
to him in the several endearing providences of his
life, which, in this, he had so illy requited the
Lord for, that broke his heart to pieces in the sense
of it; and I doubt not but some of us have sometimes found the like effects by comparing God's
ways and our own together.

4. Does communion with the Lord enlarge the
heart for obedience and service?   Surely it is as oil
to the wheels, that makes them run on freely and
nimbly in their course.   Thus, when Isaiah had obtained a special manifestation of God, and the Lord
asked, " Whom shall I send?" He presents a ready
soul for the employment, "Here am I, Lord, send
me," Isa. vi. 8.   Why, the very same effect fol-

lows sanctified providences, as you may see in
Jehoshaphat, 2 Chron. xvii. 5, 2, and in David,
Psalm cxvi. 12. O! when a soul considers what
God hath done for him, he cannot fail to say,
What shall I return? How shall I answer these
engagements?

And thus you see what sweet communion a soul
may have with God in the way of his providences.
O that you would thus walk with him! How much
of heaven might be found on earth this way! And
certainly it will never repent the Lord he hath done
you good, when his mercies produce such effects
on your hearts: he will say of every favour, thus
improved, it was well bestowed, and he will rejoice over you to do you good for ever.

Second motive. A great part of the pleasure
and delight of the Christian life is made out of the
observations of Providence. It is said, " The
works of the Lord are great, sought out of all them
that have pleasure therein," Psal. cxi. 2, that is,
the study of Providence is so sweet and pleasant,
that it invites and allures the soul to search and
dive into it. How pleasant is it to a well-tempered
soul to behold and observe

1. The sweet harmony and consent of divine
attributes in the issues of Providence! They may
seem sometimes to jar and clash, to part with each
other, and go contrary ways; but they only seem
so to do; for, in the winding up, they always
meet and embrace each other. " Mercy and truth
have met together; righteousness and peace have
kissed each other," Psal. lxxxv. 10. It is spoken
with an immediate reference to that signal providence of Israel's deliverance out of the Babylonish
captivity, and the sweet effects thereof; wherein
the truth and righteousness of God in the pro-

mises, did, as it were, kiss and embrace the mercy
and peace that were contained in the performace
of them, after they had seemed for seventy years
to be at a great distance from each other: for it is
an allusion to the usual demonstrations of joy and
gladness that two dear friends are wont to give
and receive, after a long absence and separation
from each other: they no sooner meet, but they
smile, embrace, and kiss each other. Even thus
it is here; for whenever these blessed promises
and performances meet and kiss each other, they
are also joyfully embraced and kissed by believing
souls. There is, I doubt not, a mediate reference
of this Scripture to the Messiah also, and our re-
demption by him; in him it is that these divine
attributes, which before seemed to clash and con-
tradict one another in the business of our salvation,
have a sweet agreement and accomplishment.
Truth and righteousness do in him meet with
mercy and peace, in a blessed agreement. What
a lovely sight is this! and how pleasant to behold!
O, if with Habakkuk, chap. ii. ver. 1, we would
but stand upon our watch-tower to take due observations of Providence, what rare prospects might
we have ! Luther understands it of the word of
God, as if he had said, I will look into the word,
and observe there, how God accomplisheth all
things, and brings them to pass, and how his
works are the fulfilling of his word. Others, as
Calvin, understand it of man's own retired thoughts
and meditations, wherein a man carefully observes
what purposes and designs God hath upon the
world in general, or upon himself in particular, and
how the truth and righteousness of God in the
word, work themselves through all difficulties and
impediments, and meet in the mercy, peace, and

happiness of the saints at last. Every believer, take it in which sense you will, hath his watch-tower, as well as Habakkuk ; and give me leave to say, it is an angelical employment to stand upon it, and behold the consent of God's attributes, the accomplishment of his ends, and our own happiness in the works of Providence. For this is the very joy of the angels and saints in heaven, to see God's ends wrought out, and his attributes glorified in the mercy and peace of the church, Rev. xiv. 1—3, 8.

2. And as it is a pleasant sight to see the harmony of God's attributes, so it is exceedingly pleasant to behold the resurrection of our own prayers and hopes, as from the dead. ·Why, this you may often see, if you will duly observe the works of God's providence towards you. We hope and pray for such and such mercies to the church, or to ourselves ; but God delays the accomplishment of our hopes, suspends the answer of our prayers, and seems to speak to us, as " For the vision is yet for an appointed time, but, at the end, it shall speak and not lie ; though it tarry, wait for it, because it will surely come, it will not tarry," Hab. ii. 3.   But we have no patience to wait the time of the promise, our hopes languish and die in the interim ; and we say with the despondent church, " Our hope is perished from the Lord," Lam. iii. 18.   But, O, how sweet and comfortable is it to see these prayers fulfilled, after we have given up all expectations of them !   May we not say of them as the Scripture speaks of the restoration of the Jews, it is even life from the dead ?   This was David's case, Psal. xxxi. 22, he gave up his hopes and prayers for lost, yet he lived to see the comfortable and unexpected returns of them.   And this

was the case of Job, chap. vi. 11, he had given up
all expectation of better days, and yet this man
lived to see a resurrection of all his lost comforts
with advantage. Think how that change and unexpected turn of Providence affected his soul. It
is with our hopes and prayers as with our alms :
" Cast thy bread upon the waters, for thou shalt
find it after many days," Eccles. xi. 1, or as it
was with Jacob, who had given over all hopes of
ever seeing his beloved Joseph again, but when a
strange and unexpected providence had restored
that hopeless mercy to him again, O how ravishing and transporting was it! Gen. xlvi. 29,
30.

3. What a transporting pleasure is it to behold
great blessings and advantages to us wrought by
Providence out of those very things that seem to
threaten our ruin and misery ! And yet, by duly
observing the ways of Providence, you may, to
your singular comfort, find it so. Little did Joseph
think his transportation into Egypt had been in
order to his advancement there ; yet he lived with
joy to see it, and with a thankful heart to acknowledge it, Gen. xlv. 5. Wait and observe, and you
shall assuredly find that promise, "And we know
that all things work together for good to them that
love God, to them who are the called according to
his purpose," Rom. viii. 28, working out its way
through all providences. How many times have
you been made to say as David, "It is good for
me that I have been afflicted," Psal. cxix. 71. O
what a difference have we seen between our afflictions at our first meeting with them, and our parting from them ! We have entertained them with
sighs and tears, but parted from them with joy,
blessing God for them, as the happy instruments

of our good. Thus our fears and sorrows are turned into praises and songs of thanksgiving.

4. What unspeakable comfort is it for a poor soul, that sees nothing but sin and vileness in itself, at the same time, to see what a high esteem and value the great God hath for him! This may be discerned by a due attendance to Providence, for there, a man sees goodness and mercy following him through all his days, as it is in Psal. xxiii. 6. Other men prosecute good, and it flies from them, and they can never overtake it: but goodness and mercy follow the people of God, and they cannot avoid or escape it; it gives them chase, day by day, and finds them out, even when they sometimes, by sin, put themselves out of the way of it. In all the providences that befall them, goodness and mercy pursue them. O with what a melting heart do they sometimes reflect upon these things! And will not the goodness of God be discouraged from following me, notwithstanding all my vile affronts and abuses of it in former mercies? Lord, what am I, that mercy should thus pursue me, when vengeance and wrath pursue others as good by nature as I am? It certainly argues the great esteem God hath of a man, when he thus follows him with sanctified providences, whether they be comforts or crosses, for his good; and so much is plain, from this passage; "Lord, what is man, that thou shouldst visit him every morning, and try him every moment?" Job vii. 18. Certainly God's people are his treasure, and, by this, it appears that they are so, that he withdraws not his eye from them, Job xxxvi. 7. I say not that God's favour and respect to a man may be concluded singly from his providences; but sanctified providences may very much clear it

14

to us; and when it doth so, it cannot but be matter of exceeding great joy.

5. To conclude: What is there in all this world that can give a soul such joy and comfort, as to find himself by every thing set on and furthered in his way to heaven? And yet this may be discerned by a heedful attendance to the effects and issues of Providence.

How cross soever the winds and tides of Providence at any time seem to us, yet nothing is more certain, than that they all conspire to hasten sanctified souls to God, and fit them for glory.

St. Paul knew that both his bonds and the afflictions added to them, should turn to, or finally issue in his salvation, Philip. i. 19, not that in themselves they serve to any such purpose, but as they are overruled and determined to such an end, through prayer, and the supply of the Spirit of Jesus Christ. When prayer, the external means, and the Spirit, the internal means, are joined with affections, then they become excellent means to promote salvation. And have we not with joy observed, how those very things which sense and reason tell us are opposite to our happiness, have been the most blessed instruments to promote it? How hath God blessed crosses to mortify corruption, wants to kill our wantonness, disappointments to wean us from the world! O we little think how comfortable those things will be in the review, which are so burdensome to present sense!

Third motive. In the next place, I beseech you to consider, what an effectual means the due observation of Providence will be to overpower and suppress the natural atheism that is in your hearts.

There is a natural seed of atheism in the best

hearts, and this is very much nourished by passing a rash and false judgment upon the works of Providence. When we see wicked ones prosper in the world, and godly men crushed and destroyed in the way of righteousness and integrity, it may tempt us to think that there is no advantage by religion, and all our self-denial and holiness to be little better than lost labour. Thus stood the case with good Asaph, " Behold, these are the ungodly that prosper in the world, they increase in riches," Psal. lxxiii. 12, 13. And what doth the flesh infer from thence? Why no less than the unprofitableness of the ways of holiness; " Verily I have cleansed my heart in vain, and washed my hands in innocency." This irreligious inference carnal reason was ready to draw from the dispensations of outward prosperity to wicked men; but, now, if we would heedfully observe either the signal retributions of Providence to many of them in this world, or to all of them in the world to come, O what a full confirmation is this to our faith! " The Lord is known by the judgment which he executeth," Psal. ix. 16.

The fifty-eighth Psalm contains the characters of the most prodigious sinners, whose wickedness is aggravated, by the deliberation with which it is committed, verse 2; by their habit and custom in it, verse 3; by their incorrigibleness and persistence in it, verses 4, 5; and the providence of God is there invited to destroy their power, verse 6, and that either by a gradual and sensible consumption of them, verse 7, 8, or by a sudden and unexpected stroke, verse 9. And what shall the effects of such providences be to the righteous? Why, it shall be matter of joy, verse 10, and great confirmation to their faith in God. "Verily there is a God that judgeth in the earth," verse 11.

On the contrary, how convincingly clear are those providences that demonstrate the being, wisdom, power, love, and faithfulness of God, in the supporting, preserving, and delivering of the righteous, in all their dangers, fears, and difficulties! In these things the Lord shows himself to his people, Psal. xciv. 1.

Yea, he shows himself to spiritual eyes in his providences, as clearly as the sun manifests himself by his own beams of light: "His brightness was as the light, he had horns coming out of his hand; and there was the hiding of his power," Hab. iii. 3, 4. It is spoken of the Lord's going forth for his people in their deliverance from their enemies; and then he had horns, or rays, and beams of power and mercy coming out of his hand. By his hand is meant his providential administrations and dispensations, and the horns that came out of it is nothing else but the glorious display of his attributes in those providences. How did God make himself known to his people in that signal deliverance of them out of Egypt! See Exod. vi. 3. Then he was known to them by his name Jehovah, in giving being, by his providences, to the mercies promised.

Thus, when Christ shall give his people the last and greatest deliverance from antichrist, he shall show himself to his people in a vesture dipped in blood, and his name shall be called, "The Word of God," Rev. xix. 13. His name was the Word of God before; but then he was the word revealing and discovering the promises and truths of God, now accomplishing and fulfilling them. That his name is near, his wonderful works declare, Psal. lxxv. 1.

But, more particularly, let us bring it home to our own experience. It may be, we find ourselves sometimes assaulted with atheistical thoughts : we are tempted to think God hath left all things below to the course and sway of nature, that our prayers reach him not, as it is in Lam. iii. 44, that he regards not what evils befall us. But tell me, saints, have you not enough at hand to stop the mouths of all such temptations? O do but reflect upon your own experiences, and solemnly ask your own hearts,

1. Have you never seen the all-sufficient God in the provisions he hath made for you and yours, throughout all the way that you have gone? Who was it that supplied to you whatever was needful in all your straits? Was it not the Lord? " It is he that hath given bread to them that fear him, and hath been ever mindful of his covenant," Psal. cxi. 5. O do but consider the constancy, seasonableness, and, sometimes, the extraordinariness of these provisions, and how they have been given in upon prayer; and shut your eyes, if you can, against the convincing evidence of that great truth, "He withdraweth not his eyes from the righteous," Job xxxvi. 7.

2. Have you not plainly discerned the care of God in your preservations from so many and great dangers as you have escaped, and been carried through, hitherto? How is it that you have outlived so many mortal dangers, sicknesses, accidents, designs of enemies to ruin you? It is, I presume, beyond question with you, that the very finger of God hath been in these things, and that it is by his care alone you have been preserved. When

14*

God had so signally delivered David from a dangerous disease, and the plots of enemies against
him, " by this," saith he, " I know thou favourest
me, because mine enemy doth not triumph over
me," Psal. xli. 11. He gathered from those gracious protections the care God had over him.

3. Have you not plainly discerned the hand of
God in the returns and accomplishments of your
prayers? Nothing can be more evident than this,
to men of observation. " I sought the Lord and
he heard me, and delivered me from all my fears.
They looked unto him, and were lightened, and
their faces were not ashamed. This poor man
cried, and the Lord heard him, and saved him out
of all his troubles," Psal. xxxiv. 4—6. Parallel
to this, runs the experience of thousands and ten
thousands of Christians this day: they know they
have the petitions they asked of him. The mercy
carries the very impress and stamp of the duty
upon it; so that we can say, This is the mercy,
the very mercy, I have so often sought God about.
O how satisfying and convincing are these things!

4. Have you not evidently discerned the Lord's
hand, in guiding and directing your paths to your
unforeseen advantage? Things that you never
projected for yourselves have been brought about
beyond all your thoughts. Many such things
are with God; and which of all the saints hath
not found that word verified by clear and undeniable experience, "The way of man is not in
himself," Jer. x. 23. I presume, if you will but
look over the mercies you possess this day, you
will find three to one, it may be ten to one, thus
wrought by the Lord for you. And how satisfying, beyond all arguments in the world, are these
experiences: that there is a God to whom his

people are exceedingly dear, "a God that performeth all things for them!"

5. Is it not fully convincing, that there is a God
who takes care of you, inasmuch as you have found
in all the temptations and difficulties of your lives
his promises still fulfilled, and faithfully performed
in all those conditions. I appeal to yourselves if
you have not seen that promise made good, " I
will be with him in trouble," Psal. xci. 15, and
that " God is faithful, who will not suffer you to
be tempted above what you are able : but will, with
the temptation, also make a way to escape, that ye
may be able to bear it," 1 Cor. x. 13. Have not
these been as clearly made out by Providence before your eyes as the sun at noon-day? What
room then is left for atheistical suggestions in your
breasts?

Fourth motive. The recording and recognizing
of the performances of Providence will be a singular support to faith in future exigencies. This
excellent use of it lies full in the very eye of the
text. There never befell David, in all his troubles,
a greater strait and distress than this ; and doubtless his faith had staggered, had not the considerations of former providences come in to its relief.
From this topic faith argues, and that very strongly
and conclusively. So did David's faith in many
exigencies : when he was to encounter the cham-
pion of the Philistines, it was from former providences, that he encouraged himself, 1 Sam. xvii.
37 ; and the apostle Paul improves his experiences
to the same purpose, 2 Cor. i. 9, 10. Indeed the
whole Scripture is full of it : what Christian understands not the exceeding usefulness of those
experiences he hath had, to relieve and enliven?
But I shall not satisfy myself with the common as

sertion, than which nothing is more trite in the lips
of professors, but will labour to show you, wherein
the great usefulness of our recorded experiences,
for encouraging faith, labouring under difficulties,
consists. For this purpose, I shall desire the reader
to ponder seriously these following particulars :

1. How much advantage those things have upon
our souls, which we have already felt and tasted,
beyond those which we never relished by any
former experience! What is experience but the
bringing down of the objects of faith to the adjudi-
cation and test of spiritual sense ? Now, when any
thing hath been once tasted, felt, and judged by
former experience, it is much more easily believed
and received when it occurs again. It is much
easier for faith to travel in a path that is well known
to it, having formerly trod it, than to beat out a
new one which it never trod, nor can see one step
before it. Hence it is, though there be a difficulty
in all the acts of faith, yet scarce any in comparison with the first adventure it makes upon Christ;
and the reason lies here : because in the subsequent
acts, it hath all its former experiences to aid and
encourage it; but, in the first adventure, it hath
none at all of its own; it takes a path which it
never knew before.

To trust God, without any trial or experience, is
a more noble act of faith; but, to trust him after
we have often tried him, is known to be more easy.
O it is no small advantage to a soul, in a new
plunge of distress, to be able to say, This is not
the first time I have been in these deeps, and yet
emerged out of them! Hence it was that Christ
stirred up his disciples' memories with what Providence had formerly wrought for them in a day of
straits. " O ye of little faith, why reason ye among

yourselves, because ye have brought no bread? Do ye not yet understand, neither remember?" Matt. xvi. 8—11. As if he had said, Were ye never under any strait for bread before now? Is this the first difficulty that ever your faith combatted with? No, you have felt straits, and experienced the power and care of God in supplying them before now; and, therefore, I cannot but call you men of little faith; for a very ordinary and small measure of faith, assisted with so much experience as you have had, would enable you to trust God. There is as much difference between believing before and after experience, as there is between swimming with bladders, and our first venture into the deep waters without them.

What a singular encouragement to faith do former experiences yield it, by answering all the pleas and objections of unbelief, drawn from the object of faith! Now there are two things which unbelief stumbles at in God: one is his power, the other his willingness to help.

(1.) Unbelief objects the impossibility of relief in deep distresses: "Can God furnish a table in the wilderness? Can he give bread also? Can he provide flesh for his people?" Psal. lxxviii. 19. O vile and unworthy thoughts of God! proceeding from our measuring the immense and boundless power of God by our own line and measure; because we see not which way relief should come, we conclude none is to be expected. But all these reasonings of unbelief are vanquished by a serious reflection upon our own experiences. God hath helped, therefore he can say, "his hand is not shortened," Isa. lix. 1, that is, he hath as much power and ability as formerly.

(2.) Unbelief objects against the will of God,

and questions whether he will now be gracious,
though he hath formerly been so. But after so
many experiences of his readiness to help, what
room for doubting remains? Thus Paul inferred
from the experience of what he had done, what he
could do, 2 Cor. i. 10, and so did David, 1 Sam.
xvii. 36. Indeed if a man had never experienced
the goodness of God to him, it were not so hei-
nous a sin to question his willingness to do him
good; but what place is left after such frequent
trials?

2. It gives great encouragement to faith, as it
answers the objections of unbelief, drawn from the
subject: now these objections are of two sorts
also:

(1.) Such as are drawn from our great unworthiness. How, saith unbelief, can so sinful and
vile a creature expect that ever God should do this
or that for me? It is true, we find he did great
things for Abraham, Isaac, Jacob, Moses, &c., but
these were men of eminent holiness, men who
obeyed God, and denied themselves for him, and
lived more in a day to his glory than ever I did in
all my days.

Well, but what signifies all this to a soul, that,
under all its sensible vileness and unworthiness,
hath tasted the goodness of God as well as they?
As unworthy as I am, God hath been good to me
notwithstanding; his mercy appeared first to me,
when I was worse than I am now, both in condition and disposition; and, therefore, I will still
expect the continuance of his goodness to me,
though I deserve it not. "If, when we were enemies, we were reconciled to God by the death of
his Son, how much more, being reconciled, shall
we be saved by his life?" Rom. v. 10.

(2.) Such as are drawn from the extremity of our present condition. If troubles or dangers grow to a height, and we see nothing but ruin and misery in the eye of reason before us; now unbelief becomes importunate and troublesome to the soul; now, where are thy prayers, thy hopes, yea, where is now thy God?

But all this is easily put by and avoided, by consulting our experiences in former cases. This is not the first time I have been in these straits, nor the first time I have had the same doubts and despondencies; and yet God hath carried me through all, Psal. lxxvii. 7—9. This is it that suffers not a Christian to unravel all this hopes in an hour of temptation. O how useful are these things to the people of God!

Fifth motive. The recognition of former providences will minister to your souls continual matter of praise and thanksgiving, which is the very employment of the angels in heaven, and the sweetest part of our lives on earth.

See Psal. lxi. 7, 8. If God will prepare mercy and truth for David, he will prepare praises for his God, and that daily. " By thee have I been holden up from the womb, thou art he that took me out of my mother's bowels;" (there mercies from the beginning are recognized;) " my praise shall be continually of thee," Psal. lxxi. 6. There the natural result of those recognitions is expressed.

There are five things belonging to the praise of God, and all of them have relation to his providences exercised about us. 1. A careful observation of the mercies we receive from him, Isa. xli. 17—20. This is fundamental to all praise; God cannot be glorified for the mercies we never noted. 2. A faithful remembrance of the favours received.

" Bless the Lord, O my soul, and forget not all his benefits," Psal. ciii. 2.   Hence the Lord brands the ingratitude of his people, " They soon forgat his works," Psal. cvi. 13.   3. A due appreciation and valuation of every providence that doth us good, 1 Sam. xii. 24.   That Providence that fed them in the wilderness with manna was the most remarkable providence to them ; but they not valu- ing it at its worth, God had not that praise for it which he expected, Numb. xi. 6.   4. The excita- tion of all the faculties and powers of the soul in the acknowledgment of these mercies to us.   Thus David, " Bless the Lord, O my soul ; and all that is within me bless his holy name," Psal. ciii. 1. Soul praise is the very soul of praise, this is the very fat and marrow of that thank-offering.   5. A suitable retribution for the mercies received.   This David was careful about, Psal. cxvi. 1, and the Lord taxes good Hezekiah for the neglect of it, 2 Chron. xxxii. 24, 25.   This consists in a full and hearty resignation of all to him, that we have received by providence from him ; and in our wil- lingness actually to part with all for him, when he shall remand it.

Thus you see how all the ingredients to praise have respect to Providence ; but, more particularly, I will show you, that, as all the ingredients of praise have respect to providence, so all the mo- tives and arguments, obliging and engaging souls to praise, are found therein also.   To this end, consider how the mercy and goodness of God are exhibited by Providence to excite our thankfulness.

1. That the goodness and mercy of God are let out upon his people in his providences about them: and this is the very root of praise.   It is not so much the possession that Providence gives us of

such or such comforts, as the goodness and kindness of God in the dispensing of them, that engages a gracious soul to praise. "Because thy
loving-kindness is better than life, my lips shall
praise thee," Psal. lxiii. 3. To give, maintain,
and preserve our life, are choice acts of Providence ; but to do all this in a way of grace and
loving-kindness, this is far better than the gifts
themselves. Life is but the shadow of death without it; this is the mercy that crowns all other
mercies, Psal. ciii. 4. It is this a sanctified soul
desires God would manifest in every providence
about him, Psal. xvii. 7, and what is our praising
of God else but our showing forth that loving-kindness which he showeth forth in his providences ?
Psal. xcii. 1, 2.

2. As the loving-kindness of God, manifested
in providences, is a motive to praise, so the free
and undeserved favours of God, dispensed by the
hand of Providence, oblige the soul to praise.
This was the consideration that melted David's
heart into a thankful, praising frame, even the consideration of the free and undeserved favours cast
in upon him by Providence. "What am I ! O
Lord God? and what is my father's house, that
thou hast brought me hitherto?" 2 Sam. vii. 18,
that is, to raise me by providence from a mean
condition to all this dignity: "from following
the ewes, to feed Jacob his people," Psal. lxxviii.
70, 71. O this it is that engages thankfulness!
Gen. xxxii. 10.

3. As the freeness of mercies, dispensed by providences, engageth praise, so the multitudes of
mercies heaped this way upon us, strongly oblige
the soul to thankfulness. Thus David comes be-

15

fore the Lord, encompassed with a multitude of
mercies, to praise him, Psal. v. 7. We have our
loads of mercies, and that every day, Psal. lxviii.
19. O what a rich heap will the mercies of one
day, make, being laid together!

4. As the multitudes of mercies dispensed by
Providence oblige to praise, so the tenderness of
God's mercy manifested in his providence leaves
the soul under a strong obligation to thankfulness.
We see what tender regards the Lord hath to all
our wants, straits, and burdens. " Like as a father
pitieth his children, so the Lord pitieth them that
fear him," Psal. ciii. 13. He is full of bowels, as
is signified in James v. 11. Yea, there are not
only bowels of compassion in our God, but the
tenderness of bowels like those of a mother to her
sucking child, Isa. xlix. 15. He feels all our
pains, as if the apple of his eye were touched,
Zech. ii. 8, and all this is discovered to his people
in the way of his providences with them, Psal.
cxi. 1—4. O who of all the children of God
hath not often found this in his providences? And
who can see it, and not be filled with thankfulness? All these are so many bands clapped by
Providence upon the soul to oblige it to a life of
praise. Hence it is that the prayers of the saints
are so full of thanksgivings upon these accounts;
it is sweet to recount them to the Lord in prayer;
to lie at his feet in a holy astonishment at his gracious condescension to poor worms.

Sixth motive. The due observation of providence will endear Jesus Christ, every day more
and more to your souls. Christ is the channel of
grace and mercy; through him are all the streams
of mercy that flow from God to us, and all the re-

turns of praise from us to God, 1 Cor. iii. 21—23. All things are ours, upon no other title but our being his.

Now there are six things in providence, which exceedingly endear the Lord Jesus Christ to his people ; and these are the most sweet and delicious parts of all our enjoyments.

1. The purchase of all those mercies which Providence conveys to us is by his own blood : for not only spiritual and eternal mercies, but even all our temporal ones are the acquisitions of his blood. For, as sin forfeited all, so Christ restored all these mercies to us again by his death. Sin had so shut up mercy from us, that had not Christ made an atonement by his death, we should never have obtained it to all eternity. "It is with him that God freely gives us all things," Rom. viii. 32, heaven itself, and all things needful to bring us thither, among which is principally included the tutelage and aid of Divine Providence ; so that whatever good we receive from the hand of Providence, we must put it upon the score of Christ's blood : and, when we receive it, we must say, It is the price of blood ; it is a mercy rising up out of the death of Christ ; it cost him dear, though it come to me freely; it is sweet in the possession, but costly in the acquisition. Now this is a most endearing consideration : Did Christ die that these mercies might live ? Did he pay his invaluable blood to purchase these comforts that I possess ? O what transcendent, matchless love was the love of Christ ! You have known parents who have laid out all their stock of money to purchase estates for their children ; but when did you hear of any that spent the whole stock and treasure of their blood to make a purchase for them ? If the 'ife of Christ had not

been so afflictive and sad to him, ours could not
have been so sweet and comfortable to us: it is
through his poverty we are enriched, 2 Cor. viii.
9. These sweet mercies, that are born of Providence every day, are the fruits of the travail of his
soul.

2. The sanctification of all is by our union with
Christ: it is by virtue of our union with his person that we enjoy the sanctified gifts and blessings
of Providence. All these are mercies additional
to that great mercy, CHRIST, Matt. vi. 33. They
are given with him, as in Rom. viii. 32. This is
the tenure by which we hold them, 1 Cor. iii.
21—23. What we lost in Adam, is restored again
with advantage in Christ. Immediately upon the
fall, the curse, Gen. iii. 17, seized upon all the
miserable posterity of Adam, and upon all their
comforts, outward as well as inward; and this still
lies heavy upon them. All that Providence doth
for them that are Christless is but to feed so many
poor condemned wretches, till the sentence they
are under be executed upon them; it is indeed
bountiful and openhanded to many of them, and
fills them with earthly comforts; but not one special sanctified mercy is to be found among all their
enjoyments. These gifts of Providence do but
deceive, defile, and destroy them through their
own corruptions, and, for want of union with
Christ, "the prosperity of fools shall destroy them,"
Prov. i. 32.

But when a man is once in Christ, then all providences are sanctified and sweet. "Unto the
pure all things are pure," Tit. i. 15. "A little
that a righteous man hath, is better than the treasures of many wicked," Psal. xxxvii. 16. Now,
Christ becomes a head of influence as well as of

dominion, and in all things he consults the good of his own members, Eph. i. 22.

3. The dispensation of all our comforts and mercies is by his direction and appointment. It is true, the angels are employed in the kingdom of Providence—they move the wheels; that is, are instrumental in all the revolutions in this lower world; but still they receive directions and orders from Christ, as you may see in that admirable scheme of Providence, Ezek. i. Now, what an endearing meditation is this! Whatever creature be instrumental for any good to you, it is our Lord Jesus Christ, who gave the orders and commands to that creature to do it, and without it they could have done nothing for you. It is your Head in heaven, that consults your peace and comfort on earth. These are the fruits of his care for you. So in the preventions and restraints of evil, it is he that bridles in the wrath of devils and men, he holds the reins in his own hands, Rev. ii. 10. It was the care of Christ over his poor sheep at Damascus that stopped the raging adversary, who was upon the way, designing to destroy them, Acts ix.

4. The continuation of all your mercies and comforts, outward as well as inward, is the fruit of his intercession in heaven for you. For, as the offering up of the Lamb of God, a sacrifice for sin, opened the door of mercy at first, so his appearing before God, as a lamb that had been slain, still keeps that door of mercy open, Rev. v. 6 ; Heb. ix. 24. By this his intercession, our peace and comforts are prolonged to us, Zech. i. 12, 13. Every sin we commit would put an end to the mercies we possess, were it not for that caution which is put in for us by it. " If any man sin, we

15*

have an Advocate with the Father, Jesus Christ the righteous; and he is the propitiation for our sins," 1 John ii. 1, 2. This stops all pleas, and procures new pardons for new sins. Hence it is " he saves to the uttermost," Heb. vii. 25, to the last completing act. New sins do not do away our former pardons, nor cut off our privileges settled upon us in Christ.

5. The returns and answers of all your prayers and cries to heaven, for the removing of your afflictions, or supply of your wants, are all procured and obtained for you by Jesus Christ. He is the Master of your requests, and were it not that God had respect to him, he would never regard your cries to him, nor return an answer of peace to you, how great soever your distresses should be, Rev. viii. 3, 4. It is his name that gives your prayers their acceptance, John xv. 16, because the Father can deny him nothing, therefore your prayers are not denied. Doth God condescend to hear you in the day of trouble? Doth he convince you, by your own experience, that your prayers have power with God, and do prevail? O see how much you owe to your dear Lord Jesus Christ for this high and glorious privilege!

6. The covenant of grace, in which all your comfortable enjoyments are comprised, and by which they are secured, sanctified, and sweetened to you, is made in Christ, and ratified by him between God and you. Your mercies are all comprised in this covenant, even your daily bread, Psal. cxi. 5, as well as your justification, and other spiritual mercies. It is your covenant interest that secures to you whatever it comprises, Isa. lv. 3. Hence they are called the sure mercies of David. Nay, this is it that sanctifies them, and gives them the nature

of special and peculiar mercies. One such mercy is worth a thousand common mercies; and, being sanctified and special mercies, they must needs be exceedingly sweet beyond all other mercies. On these accounts it was that David so rejoiced in his covenant interest, though laden with many afflictions, 2 Sam. xxiii. 5. But now all this hangs entirely upon Christ. The New Testament is in his blood, 1 Cor. xi. 25, and whatever mercies you reap from that covenant, you must thank the Lord Jesus Christ for them. Put all this together, and then think how such considerations will endear Christ to your souls.

Seventh motive. The due observation of Providence hath a marvellous efficacy to melt the heart, and make it thaw, and relent ingenuously before the Lord.

How can a sanctified heart do less than melt into tears, whilst it either considers the dealings of God from time to time with it, or compares the mercies received with the sins committed, or the different administrations of Providence towards itself and others?

Let a man but set himself to think deliberately and closely of the ways of Providence towards him; let him but follow the track of Providence as it hath led him all along the way that he hath gone, and if there be any principle of gracious tenderness in him, he shall meet with variety of occasions to excite and draw it forth. Reader, go back with thy serious thoughts,

1. To the beginning of the ways of God with thee, the mercies that broke out early in thy youth, even the first-born mercies from the womb of Providence, and thou wilt say, What need I go further? Here is enough not only to move, but overwhelm

my heart. "May I not, from this time, cry unto thee, My Father, thou art the Guide of my youth," Jer. iii. 4. What a critical time is the time of youth! It is the moulding age, and, ordinarily, according to the course of those leading providences, after providences do steer their course. What levity, rashness, ignorance, and strong propensions to sin and ruin accompanied that age! How many, being then left to the sway of their own lusts, run themselves into those sins and miseries which they never recover themselves from to their dying day! These, like the errors of the first concoction, are rarely rectified afterwards. Did not the Lord guide thee by his providence when but a child? Did he then preserve thee from those follies and miscarriages which blast the very blossom, and nip the bud, so that no good fruit is to be expected afterwards? Did he then cast thee into such families, or among such company and acquaintance as moulded and formed thy spirit to a better temper? Did he then direct thee into that way of employment wherein thou hast seen so large a train of happy consequences, ever since, following thee? and wilt thou not from henceforth say, "My Father, my Father, thou art the Guide of my youth!"

2. Let us but bring our thoughts close to the providences of after-times, and consider how the several changes and removes of our lives have been ordered for us: things we never foresaw nor designed (but much better for us than what we did design) have been all along ordered for us. The way of man is not in himself. God's thoughts nave not been our thoughts, nor his ways our ways. Among the eminent mercies of thy life, reader, how many of them have been mere sur-

prisals to thee! Thine own projects have been
thrust aside to make way for better things, designed
by Providence for thee.

3. Do but observe the springs and autumns of
Providence, in what order they have flourished
and faded with thee, and thou wilt find thyself
overpowered with the sense of divine wisdom and
goodness. When necessity required, such a friend
was stirred up to help thee, such a place opened
to receive thee, such a relation raised up or continued to refresh thee; and no sooner doth providence deprive thee of any of them, but either thy
need of them ceased, or some other way is opened
to thee. O the depth of God's wisdom and goodness! O the matchless tenderness of God to his
people!

4. Compare the dealings of Providence with
you, and others, yea, with others that sprung up
with you in the same generation, it may be in the
same families, and from the same parents, it may
be in families greater and more flourishing in the
world than yours, and see the difference, upon
many great accounts, it hath made between you
and them. I knew a Christian, who, after many
years' separation, was visited by his own brother,
the very sight of whom wrought upon him much as
the sight of Benjamin did upon Joseph, so that he
could not refrain to fall upon his neck, and weep
for joy; but, after a few hours spent together,
finding the spirit of his brother not only estranged
from all that is spiritual and serious, but also very
vain and profane, he hastened to his chamber, shut
the door upon him, threw himself down at the feet
of God, and, with flowing eyes and a melting
heart, admired the distinguishing grace of God,

saying, Was not Esau Jacob's brother? O grace, grace, astonishing grace!

5. Compare the carriage of Providence towards you with your own carriage towards the Lord, and it must needs melt your hearts, to find so much mercy bestowed, where so much sin hath been committed. What place did you ever live in where you cannot remember great provocations committed, and manifold mercies, notwithstanding that, received? O, with how many *notwithstandings* and *neverthelesses*, hath the Lord done you good in every place! What relation hath not been abused by sin, and yet both raised up and continued by Providence for your comfort? In every place, God hath left the marks of his goodness, and you the remembrance of your sinfulness. Give yourselves but leave to think of these things, and it is strange if your hearts relent not at the remembrance of them.

6. Do but compare your own dangers with your fears, and both with the strange outlets and doors of escape Providence hath opened, and it cannot do less than overpower you with a full sense of divine care and goodness.

There have been dark clouds seen to rise over you, judgment even at your door, sometimes threatening your life, sometimes your liberty, sometimes your estate, and sometimes your dearest relations, in whom, it may be, your life was bound up. Remember, in that day, what faintness of spirit seized you, what charges of guilt stirred up fears of the issue within you: you turned to the Lord in that distress, and hath he not made a way to escape, and delivered you from all your fears? Psal. xxxiv. 4.

O ! is your life such a continued throng, such a distracted hurry, that there is no room to be found with Christians to sit alone, and think on these things, and press these marvellous discoveries of God in his providences upon their own hearts ? Surely, might these things but lie upon our hearts, talk with our thoughts by day, and lodge with us at night, they would even force their passage down to our very veins.

Eighth motive. Due observation of Providence will both beget and secure inward tranquillity in your minds, amidst the vicissitudes and revolutions of things in this unstable, vain world.

" I will both lay me down in peace and sleep, for the Lord only maketh me to dwell in safety," Psal. iv. 8. He resolves the sinful fears of events shall not rob him of his inward quiet, nor torture his thoughts with anxious presages. He will commit all his concerns into that faithful, fatherly hand, that had hitherto wrought all things for him, and he means not to lose the comfort of one night's rest, nor bring the evil of to-morrow upon the day, but knowing in whose hand he is, wisely enjoys the sweet felicity of a resigned will.

Now this tranquillity of our minds is as much begotten and preserved by a due consideration of Providence, as by any thing whatsoever. Hence it was that our Lord Jesus Christ, when he would cure the disciples' anxious and distracting solicitudes about a livelihood, bids them consider the care Providence hath over the birds of the air and the lilies of the field, how he feeds the one and clothes the other, without any anxious care of theirs ; and would have them well consider those providences, and reason themselves into a calm and sweet composure of spirits from those considerations, Matt. vi. 25—34.

Two things destroy the peace and tranquillity of our lives; our bewailing past disappointments, or fearing future ones. But would we once learn prevision and provision to be divine prerogatives, and take notice how often Providence baffles those that pretend to them, causing the good they foresaw (according to their conjectures) coming to their hand yet to balk them, and flee from them: and the evil they thought themselves sufficiently secured from, to invade them; I say, would we consider how Providence daily baffles these pretensions of men, and asserts its own dominion, it would greatly conduce to the tranquillity of our lives.

This is a great truth, that there is no face of adversity so formidable, but, being viewed from this station, would become amicable. Now, there are several things in the consideration of Providence that naturally and kindly compose the mind of a Christian to peace, and bring it to a sweet rest, whilst events hang in a doubtful suspense.

1. The supremacy of Providence, and its incontrollable power in working. This is often seen in the good that it brings us in a way that is above the thoughts and cares of our minds, or labours of our hands. " I had not thought," said Jacob, " to have seen thy face; and lo, God hath showed me thy seed also," Gen. xlviii. 11. There is a frequent coincidence of providence in a way of surprisal, which, from no appearance, or the remotest tendency of outward causes, could be foreseen, but rather falls visibly cross to the present scheme and posture of our affairs. Nothing tends to convince

us of the vanity and folly of our own solicitudes and projections more than this doth.

2. The profound wisdom of Providence in all that it performeth for the people of God. The wheels are full of eyes, Ezek. i. 18; that is, there is an intelligent and wise Spirit who sits upon, and governs the affairs of this world.

This wisdom shines out to us in the unexpected, yea, contrary events of things. How often have we been courting some beautiful appearance that invited our senses, and with trembling shunned the formidable face of other things, when, notwithstanding, the issues of Providence have convinced us that our danger lay in what we courted, and our good in what we so studiously declined! This also is a sweet principle of peace and quiet to the Christian's mind, that he knows not but his good may be imparted in what seemed to threaten his ruin. Many were the distresses and straits of Israel in the wilderness, but all was to humble them, that he might do them good in their latter end, Deut. viii. 16. Sad and dismal was the face of that Providence which sent them out of their own land into the land of the Chaldeans; yet even this was a project to do them good, Jer. xxiv. 5. How often have we retracted our rash and headlong censures of things upon experience of this truth, and been taught to bless our afflictions and disappointments in the name of the Lord! Many a time have we kissed those troubles at parting, which we met with trembling. And what can promote peace, under doubtful providences, more effectually than this?

3. The experiences we have had throughout our lives, of the faithfulness and constancy of Providence, are of excellent use to allay and quiet our

16

hearts in any trouble that befalls us. " Hitherto
God hath helped," 1 Sam. vii. 12. We never
found him wanting to us in any case hitherto; this
is not the first strait we have been in; the first
time that our hearts and hopes have been low.
Surely he is the same God now as heretofore; his
hand is not shortened neither doth his faithfulness
fail. O recount in how great extremities former
experience hath taught you not to despair!

4. The conjectures Christians may make of the
way of Providence towards them, from what its
former methods have been towards them, are exceedingly quieting and comfortable. It is usual
with Christians to compare times with times, and
to guess at the issue of one providence by another.
The saints do know what course Providence usually holds; and, accordingly, with great probability, collect what they may expect from what, in
like cases, they have formerly observed. Christian, examine thine own heart and its former observations, and thou wilt find, as in Psal. lxxxix.
30—32, that it is usually the way of God to prepare some smart rods to correct thee, when either
thy heart hath secretly revolted from God, and is
grown vain, careless, and sensual, or when thy
steps have declined, and thou hast turned aside to
the commission of iniquity; and then when those
rods have been sanctified to humble, reduce, and
purge thy heart, it is usually observed, that those
sad providences are then upon the change, and
then the Lord changes the voice of his providence
towards thee. " Go and proclaim these words
towards the north, and say, Return thou backsliding
Israel, saith the Lord, and I will not cause mine
anger to fall upon you, for I am merciful, saith the
Lord, and I will not keep anger for ever. Only

acknowledge thine iniquity," &c., Jer. iii. 12, 13.

If, therefore, I find the blessed effects of the rod upon me, that it hath done its work to break the hard heart, and pull down the proud heart, and awaken the drowsy heart, and quicken the slothful, negligent, lazy heart; now with great probability, I may conjecture a more comfortable aspect of Providence will quickly appear, the refreshing and reviving time is nigh.

5. It is usual with Christians to argue themselves into fresh reviving hopes, when the state of things is most forlorn, by comparing the providences of God one with another.

(1.) It is a mighty composing meditation, when we compare the providences of God towards the inanimate and irrational creatures, with his providences towards us. Doth he take care for the very fowls of the air, for whom no man provides, as well as those at the door which we daily feed? Doth he so clothe the very grass of the field? hear the young ravens when they cry for meat? and can it be supposed he should forget his own people, who are of much more value than these?

(2.) Or if we compare the bounty and care that Providence hath expressed to the enemies of God, how it feeds, and clothes, and protects them, even whilst they are fighting against him with his own mercies, it cannot but quiet and satisfy us, that, surely, he will not be wanting to that people upon whom he hath set his love, to whom he hath given his Son, and for whom he hath designed heaven itself.

(3.) It must needs quiet us, when we consider what the Lord did for us in the way of his providence, when we ourselves were in the state of na-

ture and enmity against God. Did he not then
look after us, when we knew him not? provided
for us, when we owned him not in any of his mercies? Bestowed thousands of mercies upon us,
when we had no title to Christ, nor any one promise? And will he now do less for us, since we
are reconciled and become his children?

Surely such considerations as these cannot but
fill the soul with peace, and preserve the tranquillity
of it, under the most distracting providences.

Ninth motive. Due observations of the ways
of God, in his providences towards us, have an excellent usefulness and aptitude to advance and improve holiness in our hearts and lives; for,

1. The holiness of God is manifested to us in all
his works of providence. "The Lord is righteous
in all his ways, and holy in all his works," Psal.
cxlv. 17. The instruments used by Providence
may be very sinful and wicked; they may aim at
base ends, and make use of wicked mediums to
attain them; but it is certain God's designs are
most pure, and all his workings are so too. Though
he permits, limits, orders, and overrules many
unholy persons and actions, yet, in all, he works
like himself, and his holiness is no more defiled
and stained by their impurity, than the sunbeams
are by the noisome exhalations of a dunghill.
"He is the rock, his work is perfect; for all his
ways are judgment, a God of truth, and without
iniquity; just and right is he," Deut. xxxii. 4.
So that in all his providences he sets before us a
perfect pattern of holiness, that he might be holy
in all our ways, as our Father is in all his ways.
But this is not all.

2. His providences, if duly observed, promote
holiness by stopping up our way to sin. O! if

men would but note the designs of God in his preventive providences, how useful would it be to
keep them upright and holy in their ways! For
why is it that the Lord so often hedges up our way
with thorns, as it is in Hosea ii. 6, but that we
should not find our paths to sin? Why doth he
clog us, but to prevent our straying from him?
"Lest I should be exalted above measure, there
was given me a thorn in the flesh, a messenger of
Satan to buffet me," 2 Cor. xii. 7.   O! it is good
to attend to these works of God, and study the
meaning of them.   Sometimes Providence crosses
a hopeful, thriving project to advance our estate,
and frustrates all our labours and cares; why is
this, but to hide pride from man? Shouldst thou
prosper in the world, that prosperity might be thy
snare, and make thee a proud, sensual, vain soul;
the Lord Jesus sees this, and therefore withdraws
the food and fuel from thy corruptions.

It may be thou hast a diseased, weak body;
thou labourest often under infirmities: in this the
wisdom and care of God over thy soul is manifested; for wert thou not so clogged, how probable is it that much more guilt might be contracted! Your poverty doth but clog your pride;
reproaches clog your ambition; want prevents
wantonness; sickness of body conduces to the
prevention of many inward stings of conscience,
and groans under guilt.

3. The providences of God may be observed to
conduce to our holiness, not only preventing sin,
that we may not fall into it, but also purging our
sins when we are fallen into them.*   "By this,

---

* God would not suffer instruments to rub so hard,
if it were not to fetch out the dirt that is engrained in

16*

therefore, shall the iniquity of Jacob be purged;
and this is all the fruit, to take away his sin," Isa.
xxvii. 9, and so Dan. xi. 33—35; they are of the
same use that fire and water are for purging and
cleansing; not that they can purge us from sin in
their own virtue and power, for, if so, those that
have most afflictions would have most grace also;
but it is in the virtue of Christ's blood, and God's
blessing upon afflictive providences, that they purge
us from sin. A cross without a Christ never did
any man good. Now, in God's afflictive providences for sin, there are many things that tend to
the purging of it: for,

(1.) Such rebukes of Providence discover the
displeasure of God against us; the Lord frowns
upon us in those providences: our Father is angry,
and these are the tokens of it; and nothing works
more to the melting of a gracious heart than this.
Must not the heart of a child melt and break whilst
the father is angry? O this is more bitter to our
spirits, than all the smart and anguish of the affliction can be to our flesh! "O Lord, rebuke me
not in thy wrath; neither chasten me in thy hot
displeasure: for thine arrows stick fast in me;
and thine hand presseth me sore. There is no
soundness in my flesh, because of thine anger:
neither is there any rest in my bones, because of
my sin," Psalm xxxviii. 1—3.

(2.) By these rebukes for sin, the evil of sin is
discovered more sensibly to us, and we are made
to see more clearly the evil of it in these glasses of
affliction which Providence at such times sets be-

our natures. He loves purity so well, he had rather
see a hole than a spot in his child's garment.—*Gur-
nall's Christian Armour.* Par. 2. p. 221.

fore us, than formerly we ever saw. "Thine own wickedness shall correct thee, and thy back-slidings shall reprove thee : know, therefore, and see that it is an evil thing and bitter, that thou hast forsaken the Lord thy God, and that my fear is not in thee, saith the Lord God of hosts," Jer. ii. 19. O the gall and wormwood that we taste in it under God's rebukes for it!

(3.) Providence blasts and frustrates all sinful projects to the people of God ; whoever thrives in them, they shall not, Isa. xxx. 1—5. And this also convinces them of the folly that is in sin, and makes them cleave to the way of simplicity and integrity.

(4.) Holiness is promoted in the soul, by caution-ing and warning the soul against sin for time to come. " I have borne chastisements, I will not offend any more," Job xxxiv. 31. O happy pro-vidences, how smart soever, that make the soul for ever afraid of sin! Surely such rods are well be-stowed. This gives God his end ; and if ever we sorrowed after a godly sort in the day of our troubles, it will work this carefulness. " Behold this self-same thing that ye sorrowed after a godly sort, what carefulness it wrought in you," &c., 2 Cor. vii. 11. O, if ever a man have been under a sanctified rod, which hath showed him the evil of sin, and kindly humbled him for it, and a temp-tation should again solicit him to the same evil : Why, thinks he, what a madness is it for me to buy repentance at so dear a rate! Have I not smarted enough already? You may as well ask me, whether I shall run again into the fire, after I have been already scorched in it.

(5.) Providences do greatly improve and promote holiness by drawing the soul into the presence of

God, and giving it the opportunity and occasion of much communion with him. Comfortable providences will do this, they will melt a man's heart in love to the God of his mercies, and so pain his heart that he shall not be quiet till he have found a place to pour out his soul in thankfulness to the Lord, 2 Sam. vii. 18.

Afflictive providences will drive us to the feet of God, and there make us to judge and condemn ourselves ; and all this hath an excellent use to destroy sin, and promote holiness in the soul.

Tenth motive. Lastly, the consideration and study of providence will be of singular use to us in a dying hour. Hereby we treasure up that which will singularly sweeten our death to us, and greatly assist our faith in the last encounter. We find, when Jacob died, what reflections he had upon the dealings of God with him in the various providences of his life. See Gen. xlviii. 3. 7. 15, 16. In like manner you find Joshua recording the providences of God, when at the brink of the grave; they were the subject of his dying discourse, Josh. xxiv., and I cannot but think it a sweet close to the life of any Christian : it must needs sweeten a death-bed, to recount there the several remarkable passages of God's care and love to us from our beginning to that day ; to reflect upon the mercies that went along with us all the way, when we are come to the end of it. O Christians, treasure up these instances for such a time as that is, that you may go out of the world blessing God for all the goodness of truth he hath performed to you all your life long. Now the meditations of these things must needs be of great use in that day, if you consider the following particulars :

1. The time of death is the time when souls are

usually most violently assaulted by Satan, with
horrid temptations and black suggestions.   We
may say of that figuratively, as it is said of the
natural serpent, he never exerts his utmost rage till
the last encounter, and then his great design is to
persuade the saints that God loves them not, hath
no care nor regard for them, nor their cries; though
they pray for ease, and cry for sparing mercy, they
see none comes.   He handles them with as much
roughness and severity as other men; yea, many
of the vilest and most dissolute wretches endure
less torments and are more gently handled than
they. "There are no bands in their death,"
Psal, lxxiii. 4, whereas thou must go through a
long lane of sickness to the grave, and endure
many deaths in one.

But what credit can these plausible tales of Satan obtain with a Christian, who hath been treasur-
ing up all his life long the memories of God's
tender regard, both to his wants and prayers, and
that hath carefully remarked the evident returns of
his prayers, and gracious condescensions of God to
him, from his beginning to that moment?   In this
case, his faith is mightily assisted by thousands of
experiences which back and encourage it, and will
not suffer the soul to give up so easily a truth which
he hath so often sensibly felt and tasted.   I am
sure, saith he, God hath had a tender, fatherly
care of me ever since I became his; he never failed
me yet in any former strait, and I cannot believe
he will do so now.   I know his love is like himself,
unchangeable.   "Having loved his own which
were in the world, he loved them unto the end,"
John xiii. 1.   "For this God is our God for ever
and ever, he will be our Guide, even unto death,"
Psal. xlviii. 14.   Did he love me in my youth, and

will he cast me off in my decrepid age? "O God," says the Psalmist, " thou hast taught me from my youth, and hitherto have I declared thy wondrous works; now also, when I am old and grey-headed, O God, forsake me not," Psalm lxxi. 17, 18.

2. At death, the saints are engaged in the last and one of the most eminent works of faith, even the committing of themselves into the hands of God, when we are launching forth into that vast eternity, and entering into that new state, which will make so great a change upon us in a moment. In this, Christ sets us a pattern; "Father, into thy hands I commend my spirit," Luke xxiii. 46, and having said thus, he gave up the ghost. So Stephen, at his death, " Lord Jesus, receive my spirit, and immediately fell asleep," Acts vii. 59, 60.

There are two signal and remarkable acts of faith, both exceedingly difficult, namely, its first act and its last. The first is a great venture that it makes of itself upon Christ; and the last is a great venture too, to cast itself into the ocean of eternity, upon the credit of a promise. But yet I know the first adventure of the soul upon Christ is much more difficult than the last adventure upon death; and that which makes it so is, in a great measure, the manifold recorded experiences that the soul hath been gathering up from the day of its espousals to Christ, unto its dying-day, which is, in a sense, its marriage-day. O! with what encouragement may a soul throw himself into the arms of that God, with whom he hath so long conversed and walked, in this world! whose visits have been sweet and frequent, with whom the soul hath contracted so intimate acquaintance in this world; whom he hath committed all his affairs to, former-

,y, and still found him a faithful God; and now hath no reason to doubt but he shall find him so in this last distress and exigence also.

3. At death, the people of God receive the last mercies that ever they shall receive in this world by the hand of Providence, and are immediately to make up their accounts with God, for all the mercies that ever they received from his hand. What can be more suitable, therefore, to a dying person, than to recount with himself the mercies of his whole life, the manifold receipts of favour for which he is to reckon with God, speedily; and how shall this be done without a due and serious observation and recording of them now? I know there are thousands of mercies forgotten by the best of Christians; a memory of brass cannot contain them: and I know also that Jesus Christ must make up the account for us, or it will never pass with God; yet it is our duty to keep the accounts of our mercies, and how they have been improved by us, for we are stewards, and then we are to give an account of our stewardship.

4. At death, we owe an account also to men, and stand obliged, if there be opportunity for it, to make known to them that survive us, what we have seen and found of God in this world that we may leave a testimony for God with men, and bring up a good report upon his ways. Thus dying Jacob, when Joseph was come to take his last farewell of him in this world, strengthened himself, and sat upon the bed, and related to him the eminent appearances of God to him, and the places where, Gen. xlviii. 2, 3, as also an account of his afflictions, ver. 7. So Joshua, in his last speech to the people, makes it his business to vindicate and clear the truth of the promises, by re-

counting to them how the providence of God hath
fulfilled the same, to a tittle, in his day. "And
behold," saith he, "this day I am going the way
of all the earth, and ye know in all your hearts,
and in all your souls, that not one thing hath failed
of all the good things which the Lord your God
spake concerning you; all are come to pass unto
you, and not one thing hath failed thereof," Joshua
xxiii. 14.

And certainly it is of great importance to the
world to understand the judgments, and hear of
the experiences of dying men. They, of all men,
are presumed to be most wise and most serious;
besides, this is the last opportunity that ever we
shall have in this world to speak of God. O,
then, what a sweet thing would it be to close up
our lives with an honourable account of the ways
of God! To go out of the world blessing him for
all the mercies and truth which he hath here performed to us! How would this encourage weak
Christians, and convince the atheistical world that
verily there is a reality and an excellency in the
ways and people of God!

5. At death, we begin the angelical life of praise
and thanksgiving: we then enter upon that everlasting sweet employment; and, as I doubt not but
the providences in which we were concerned in
this world will be a part of that song which we
shall sing in heaven, so certainly it will become
us to tune our hearts and tongues for it, whilst we
are here, and especially when we are ready to
enter upon that blessed state. Let it, therefore, be
your daily meditation and study, what God hath
been to you, and done for you, from the beginning
of his way hitherto.

And thus I have spread before you some encouragements to this blessed work. O that you would be persuaded to this lovely and every way beneficial practice! This I dare presume to say, that whoever finds a careful and a thankful heart, to record and treasure up the daily experiences of God's mercy to him, shall never want new mercies to record, to his dying day. It was said of Claudian, that he wanted matter suitable to the excellence of his parts; but where is the head or heart that is suitable to this matter? Who can utter the mighty acts of the Lord? Who can show forth all his praise? Psal. cvi. 2.

Thus I have, through the aid of Providence, despatched the main design I aimed at in the choice of this subject. All that remains will now be speedily finished in some few corollaries to be briefly noted upon the whole, and three or four practical cases to be stated. You have heard how Providence " performeth all things for you." Learn hence,

First corollary. That God is therefore to be owned by you in all that befalls you in this world, whether it be in a way of success and comfort, or of trouble and affliction. O, it is your duty to observe his hand and disposal! When God gives you comforts, it is your great evil not to observe his hand in them. Hence was the charge against Israel, " She did not know that I gave her corn, and wine, and oil, and multiplied her silver and gold," Hos. ii. 8, that is, she did not actually and affectionately consider my care over her, and goodness to her in these mercies. And so for afflictions, it is a great wickedness, when God's hand is lifted up, not to see it, Isa. xxvi. 11. " The ox knoweth his owner, and the ass his master's crib," Isa. i. 3; the most dull and stupid creatures

17

know their benefactors. O look to the hand of
God in all, and know, that neither your comforts
nor afflictions arise out of the dust, or spring up
out of the ground.

Second corollary. If God perform all things
for you, how great is his condescension to and care
over his people! " What is man that thou shouldst
magnify him, and set thine heart upon him? and
that thou shouldst visit him every morning, and
try him every moment?" Job vii. 17, 18. Such
is his tender care over you, that he withdraws not
his eye from you. See Job xxxvi. 7. Lest any
hurt you, he himself will guard and keep you, day
and night, Isa. xxvii. 3. Should he withdraw his
eye or hand one moment from you, that moment
would be your ruin. Ten thousand evils watch
but for such an opportunity to rush in upon you,
and destroy you and all your comforts. You are
too dear to him to be trusted in any hand but his
own. " All his saints are in thy hand," Deut.
xxxiii. 3.

Third corollary. Learn hence how you are
obliged to perform all duties and services for God,
who performeth all things for you. It was the
wish of a good man, O! that I could be to God
what my hand is to me, namely, a serviceable,
useful instrument! Shall God do all things for you,
and will you do nothing for God? Is Providence
every moment at work for you, and will you be
idle? To what purpose then is all that God hath
done for you? Is it not the aim and design of all
to make you a fruitful people? If God plant, and
fence, and water you by providence, surely he
looks you should bring forth fruit, Isa. v. 1—4.
O that, in return for all the benefits of Providence,
you would say to God, as grateful Elisha said to

the Shunammite, Behold thou hast been careful for
us with all this care, what is to be done for thee?
2 Kings iv. 13, and with David, "What shall I
render unto the Lord for all his benefits towards
me?" Psal. cxvi. 12.   He is ever doing you good,
be you always abounding in his work.   His providence stands by you in your greatest distresses
and dangers; do not you flinch from God, when
his service and your duty is compassed about with
difficulties.   O be active for that God who is acting
every moment for you!

Fourth corollary.   Doth God perform all things
for his people?   Do not distrust him then as often
as new or great difficulties arise.   Why should
you think that He who hath done so many things
for you will now do no more?   Surely " the Lord's
hand is not shortened that it cannot save, nor his
ear heavy, that it cannot hear," Isa. lix. 1.   If any
thing put a stop to his mercy, it is your iniquities,
your distrust, and infidelity.   "How long will it
be ere you believe him?"   If a thousand and ten
thousand trials and experiences of his tender care,
faithfulness, and love, will cure this distemper in
you, you have them at hand to do it.   If the frequent confutations of this your distrust, by the unexpected breakings-out of mercy for you, under
like discouragements, will cure it, look back, and
you may see them.   Certainly you have been
often forced by Providence, with shame and repentance, to retract your rash censures of his care!
and yet will you fall into the same distemper
again?   O, that you would once learn this great
truth, that no man ever wanted that mercy, which
he wanted not a heart to trust and wait quietly
upon God for.   You never yet sought God in vain,
except when you sought him vainly.

Fifth corollary. Doth God perform all things for you? Then seek God for all by prayer, and never undertake any design without him: certainly, if he do not perform it for you, you can never have what you desire and labour for: and though he have designed to perform this or that mercy for you, yet for these things he will be inquired of, that he may do it for you, Ezek. xxxvi. 37. I reckon that business as good as done, that mercy as good as if it were in hand, that trouble as good as over, for the doing, enjoying, or removing whereof we have engaged God by prayer. It is our folly to engage this instrument or that for us, to attempt this way and that way to compass our design, and all the while forget Him, upon whose pleasure all instruments and means entirely depend. That which begins not with prayer, seldom winds up with comfort. " The way of man is not in himself;" if it were, prayer might then be reckoned lost labour. O let Him that performs all, be owned and acknowledged in all.

Sixth corollary. Lastly, if God perform all things for us; then it is our great interest and concern in all things to study to please him, upon whom we depend for all things.

It is a grave and weighty observation of Chrysostom: Nothing should be grievous and bitter to a Christian, but to provoke the displeasure of God. Avoid that, and no affliction or trouble whatever can cast down such a prudent soul; but even as a spark is easily extinguished in the sea, so will the favour of God extinguish all those troubles. It is with such a soul, saith he, as it is with the heavens, we think the heavens suffer, when they are overspread with clouds, and the sun suffers when t is eclipsed; but there is no such thing, they suffer not when they seem to suffer. Every thing is well, and shall be well, when all is well between us and God. The great consolation of the saints lies in this, that all which concerns them is in the hands of their Father. " I had utterly despaired," saith Luther, "had Christ not been head of the church." When he that performs all things is our God, even our God that delights in our prosperity, that rejoices over us to do us good, what ample security is there in the greatest confusions and dangers. When one told Borromeus, that there were some that laid wait for his life, his answer was, What! is God in the world for nothing? And as notable was the reply of Silentiarius in a like case, If God takes no care of me, how do I live, how have I subsisted hitherto? Though it seem a romance to many, saith a late grave author, yet we must either quit the Scriptures or give credit to this, that the most infallible rules for one to raise his fortune and insure a destiny, that can control the stars, are given forth there, namely, in the Scriptures, where it is evidently found, that a good man may even be his own carver. O that we would but steer our course according to those rare politics of the Bible, those divine maxims of wisdom! Fear nothing but sin. Study nothing so much as how to please God. Warp not from your integrity under any temptation. Trust God in the way of your duty. These are sure rules to secure yourselves and your interest in all the vicissitudes of this life.

My last work will be to state three or four practical cases about this subject, and so I shall shut up this discourse of Providence.

First case. How may a Christian discover the
17*

will of God and his own duty, under dark and
doubtful providences?

In order to the clearing of this case, we are to
consider what is meant by the will of God; what
by those doubtful providences, that make the discovery of his will difficult; and what rules are to
be observed for the clearing up of God's will to
ourselves, under such difficult and puzzling providences.

As to the will of God, it falls under a twofold
consideration, namely, of his secret and revealed
will. This distinction is found in that Scripture,
" The secret things belong unto the Lord our God,
but those things which are revealed belong unto
us," &c., Deut. xxix. 29. The first is the rule of
his own actions, the latter of ours; and this only
is concerned in the query.

This revealed will of God is either manifested to
us in his word, or in his works. The former is
his commanding will; the latter, his effecting or
permitting will; the one concerning good; the
other, about evil.

In these ways God manifests his will to men,
but yet with great variety and difference, both as to
the things revealed, the persons to whom he reveals them, and the degrees of clearness in which
they are revealed. 1. As to the things revealed,
there is great difference; for the great and necessary duties of religion are revealed to us in the word
with great perspicuity and evidence. About these,
there can be no hesitation; but things of a lower
nature and lesser concern are left more obscure.
2. As to the persons to whom God reveals his will,
there is great difference; some are strong men,
others babes, 1 Cor. iii. 1; some have senses ex-

ercised, others are of weak and dull understanding; and we know every thing is received according to the ability and measure of the person receiving it. Hence it is, that one man's way is very plain before him, he knows what he ought to do; the other is ever and anon at a loss, dubious and uncertain what to do. 3. The manner of God's revealing his will to men is also very different. Some have had special, personal, and peculiar discoveries of it made to them. So had Samuel about the choice of the person whom he should anoint king, 1 Sam. ix. 15, and so had David, 1 Sam. xxiii. 2, 4, 9—12: where you find, upon his inquiry of God, (likely by the *urim* and *thummim*,) God told him what was his duty as to that expedition, and what would be the event of it.

But now all are tied up to the ordinary, standing rule of the written word, and must not expect any such extraordinary revelations from God. The way we now have to know the will of God concerning us in difficult cases, is to search and study the Scriptures; and where we find no particular rule to guide us in this or that particular case, there we are to apply general rules, and govern ourselves according to the analogy and proportion they bear towards each other.

But now, it often falls out, that in such doubtful cases we are entangled in our own thoughts, and put to a loss what course to take. We pray with David, that God would "make his way plain before us," Psal. v. 8. Afraid we are of displeasing God, and yet doubtful we may do so, whether we resolve this way or that. And this comes to pass, not only through the difficulty of the case, and from our own ignorance and inadvertency, but very frequently from those providences that lie before us,

wherein God seems to hint his mind to us, this way
or that; or whether we may safely guide ourselves, by those intimations of Providence, is doubtful to us.

That God doth give men secret hints and intimations of his will, by his providence, cannot be
doubted; but yet providences, in themselves, are
no stable rule of duty, nor sufficient discovery of
the will of God.   We may say of them, " Behold,
I go forward, but he is not there: and backward,
but I cannot perceive him : on the left hand, where
he doth work, but I cannot behold him ; he hideth
himself on the right hand, that I cannot see him,"
Job xxiii. 8, 9.

If providence in itself be allowed to be a sufficient discovery of God's will to us, then we shall
be forced oftentimes to justify and condemn the
same cause or person, forasmuch as there is " one
event happens to all," and as it falls out to the
good, so to the wicked, Eccles. ix. 2.   Besides, if
providence alone were the rule to judge any action
or design by, then a wicked undertaking would
cease to be so, if it should succeed well ; but sin is
sin still, and duty is duty still, whatever the events
and issues of either be.

The safest way, therefore, to make use of providences, in such cases, is to consider them as
they follow the commands or promises of the word,
and not singly or separately in themselves.   If
you search the Scriptures with an impartial and
unbiased spirit, in a doubtful case, pray for counsel and direction from the Lord, attend to the dictates of conscience ; when you have done all, and
shall find the providences of God falling out agree-
ably to the dictates of your own conscience, and
the best light you can find in the word, you may,

in such cases, make use of it as an encouragement
to you in the way of your duty; but the most signal
demonstrations of Providence are not to be accepted
against a Scripture rule; no smiles or successes of
Providence may in this case encourage us to proceed : and, on the other side, no frowns or discouragements of Providence should dishearten us
in the way of our duty, how many soever we
should encounter therein.   Holy Job could not
find the meaning of God in his works, yet would
he not " go back from the commandment of his
lips," Job xxiii. 12.   The like resolution you find
in David to proceed in his duty, and cleave to the
word, how many stumbling-blocks soever Providence should permit to be laid in his way.   "I
am become," saith he, "like a bottle in the smoke,"
not only blacked, but withered up by troubles, "yet
do I not forget thy statutes," Psal. cxix. 83; and
again, " They had almost consumed me upon
earth; but I forsook not thy precepts," ver. 87.

Paul, by the direction of the Spirit, was engaged
to go to Jerusalem, Acts xx. 22.   After a clear re-
velation of the mind of God to him in that matter,
how many difficult and discouraging providences
befell him in his way!   The disciples of Tyre
said to him " by the Spirit," though in that they
followed their own spirits, " that he should not go
to Jerusalem," Acts xxi. 4.

Then at Cesarea, he met Agabus, a prophet, who
told him what should befall him when he came
thither, Acts xxi. 10, 11.   All this will not dis-
suade him.   And after all this, how passionately
do the brethren beseech him to decline that journey! verses 12, 13.   Yet knowing his rule, and
resolving to be faithful to do it, he puts by all, and
proceeds on in his journey.

Well then, Providence, in concurrence with the word, may give some encouragement to us in our way, but no testimony of Providence is to be accepted against the word. If Scripture and conscience tell you, such a way is sinful, you may not venture upon it, how many opportunities and encouragements soever Providence may suffer to offer themselves to you, for they are only permitted for your trial, not your encouragement: take this, therefore, for a sure rule, that no providence can legitimate or justify any moral evil; nor will it be a plea before God, for any man to say, The providence of God gave me encouragement to do it, though the word gave me none. If, therefore, in doubtful cases, you would discover God's will, govern yourselves in your search after it by these rules.

1. Get the true fear of God upon your hearts; be really afraid of offending him; God will not hide his mind from such a soul. "The secret of the Lord is with them that fear him, and he will show them his covenant," Psal. xxv. 14.

2. Study the word more, and the concerns and interests of the world less. The word is a light to your feet, Psal. cxix. 105, that is, it hath a discovering and directive usefulness as to all the duties to be done, and dangers to be avoided: it is a great oracle at which you are to inquire: treasure up its rules in your hearts, and you will walk safely. "Thy word have I hid in my heart, that I might not sin against thee," Psal. cxix. 11.

3. Reduce what you know into practice, and you shall know what is your duty to practise. "If any man do his will, he shall know of the doctrine," John vii. 17. "A good understanding

have all they that do his commandments," Psal.
cxi. 10.

4. Pray for illumination and direction in the
way that you should go; beg the Lord to guide
you in straits, and that he would not suffer you
to fall into sin. This was the holy practice of
Ezra. "Then I proclaimed a fast there at the
river Ahava, that we might afflict ourselves before
our God, to seek of him a right way for us, and
for our little ones, and for all our substance,"
Ezra viii. 21.

5. And this being done, follow providence so
far as it agrees with the word, and no further.
There is no use to be made of providence against
the word, but in subserviency to it; and there are
two excellent uses of providence in subserviency
to the word. 1. Providences as they follow promises and prayer, are evidences of God's faithfulness in their accomplishment. When David lan-
guished under a disease, and his enemies began to
triumph in the hopes of his downfall, he prays
that God would be merciful to him, and raise him
up; and by that, he saith, "He knew the Lord
favoured him, because his enemy did not triumph
over him," Psal. xli. 11. This providence he
looks upon as a token for good, as elsewhere he
calls it, Psal. lxxxvi. 17. 2. Providences give us
loud calls to those duties, which the command lays
upon us, and tell us when we are actually and
presently under the obligation of the commands as
to the performance of them. Thus, when sad providences befall the church or ourselves, they call
us to humiliation, and let us know that then the
command to humble ourselves at the feet of God
is in force upon us. "The Lord's voice crieth to

the city and the man of wisdom shall see thy
name, hear the rod, and who hath appointed it,"
Micah vi. 9. The rod hath a voice, and what
doth it speak? Why now is the time to humble
yourselves under the mighty hand of God; this is
the day of trouble in which God hath bid you to
call upon him; and, contrariwise, when comfortable providences refresh us, it now informs us,
this is the time to rejoice in God, according to the
rule: " In the day of prosperity be joyful," Eccles.
vii. 14. These precepts bind always, but apply
to various circumstances: it is our duty, therefore,
and our wisdom, to distinguish seasons, and know
the proper duties of every season; and Providence
is an index that points them out to us.

Second case. How may a Christian be supported in waiting upon God, whilst Providence
delays the performance of the mercies to him, for
which he hath long prayed and waited?

Two things are supposed in this case. That
Providence may linger and delay the performance
of those mercies to us, that we have long waited
and prayed for; that during that delay and suspension, our hearts and hopes may be very low,
and ready to fail.

1. Providence may long delay the performance
of those mercies we have prayed and waited upon
God for.

For the right understanding of this, know that
there is a twofold term, or season, fixed for the
performance of mercy to us. One by the Lord
our God, in whose hand times and seasons are,
Acts i. 7; another by ourselves, who raised up our
own expectations of mercies, sometimes merely
through the eagerness of our desires after them,

and sometimes upon uncertain conjectural grounds and appearances of encouragement, that lie before us.

Now, nothing can be more precise, certain, and punctual, than is the performance of mercy at the time and season which God hath appointed, how long soever it be, or how many obstacles soever lie in the way of it. There was a time prefixed by God himself for the performance of that promise of Israel's deliverance out of Egypt; and it is said, " At the end of the four hundred and thirty years, even the self-same day, it came to pass that all the host of the Lord went out of the land of Egypt," Exod. xii. 41. Compare this with Acts vii. 17, and there you have the ground and reason why their deliverance was not, nor could be, delayed one day longer, because " the time of the promise was now come." Promises must accomplish their appointed time, and when they have so done, Providence will fulfil them, and not one of them shall miscarry.

But for the seasons, which are of our own fixing and appointment, as God is not tied to them, so his providences are not governed by them, and hence are our disappointments. " We looked for peace, but no good came; for a time of health, and behold trouble," Jer. viii. 15. And hereupon is it that we fret at the delays of Providence, and suspect the faithfulness of God in their performance. " But his thoughts are not our thoughts," Isa. lv. 8. " The Lord is not slack concerning his promise, as men count slackness," 2 Pet. iii. 9. It is slackness, if you reckon by our own rule and measure, but it is not so if you reckon and count it by God's. The Lord doth not compute and reckon his seasons of working by our arithmetic.

You have both these rules compared, and the ground of our mistake detected in this Scripture: "The vision is yet for an appointed time, but, at the end, it shall speak, and not lie: though it tarry, wait for it, because it will surely come, it will not tarry," Hab. ii. 3.

God appoints the time: when that appointed time is come, the expected mercies will not fail; but, in the mean time, "though it tarry," saith the prophet, "wait for it, for it will not tarry." Tarry, and not tarry, how shall this be reconciled? The meaning is, it may tarry much beyond your expectation, but not a moment beyond God's appointment.

2. During this delay of Providence, the hearts and hopes of the people of God may be very low, and much discouraged. This is very plain from what the Scriptures have recorded of others, and every one of us may find in our own experiences. We have an instance of this in Isa. xlix. 13, 14. In the 13th verse you have God's faithful promise, that "he will comfort his people, and have mercy upon his afflicted;" enough, one would think, to raise and comfort their hearts. But the mercy promised was long in coming, they waited from year to year, and still the burden pressed them, and was not removed. And therefore "Zion said, the Lord hath forsaken me, and my Lord hath forgotten me," ver. 14, as if she had said, It is in vain to look for such a mercy, God hath no regard to us, we are out of his heart and mind, he neither cares for us, nor minds what becomes of us.

So it was with David, after God had made him such a promise, and in the time thereof so faithfully performed it, that never was mercy better secured to any man; for they are called "the sure mercies of David," Isa. lv. 3, yet Providence delayed the accomplishment of them so long, and suffered such difficulties to intervene, that he not only despairs to see the accomplishment of them, but even concludes God had forgotten them too. "How long wilt thou forget me, O Lord? for ever?" Psal. xiii. 1. And what he speaks here by way of question, he elsewhere turns into a positive conclusion: "All men are liars; I shall one day perish by the hand of Saul," Psal. cxvi. 11. And the causes of these despondencies and sinkings of heart are partly from ourselves, and partly from Satan. If we duly examine our own hearts about it, we shall find that these sinkings of heart are,

(1.) The immediate effects of unbelief. We do not depend and rely upon the word with that full trust and confidence that are due to the infallible word of a faithful and unchangeable God. You may see the ground of this faintness in that Scripture, "I had fainted unless I had believed," Psal. xxvii. 13. Faith is the only cordial that relieves the heart against these faintings and despondencies. Where this is wanting, or is weak, no wonder our hearts sink at this rate, when discouragements are before us.

(2.) Our judging and measuring things by the rules of sense; this is a great cause of our discouragements. We conclude, that according to the appearances of things, so will be their issues. If Abraham had done so in that great trial of his faith, he had certainly lost his footing; "but against hope (that is, against natural probability) he believed in hope, giving glory to God," Rom. iv. 18. If Paul had done so, he had fainted under his trials. "We faint not," saith he, "whilst we look not at

the things that are seen," 2 Cor. iv. 16, 18, as if
he had said, that which keeps up our spirits is our
looking off from things present and visible, and
measuring all by another rule, namely, the power
and fidelity of God firmly engaged in the promises.

(3.) In all these things, Satan manages a design
upon us.   Hence he takes occasion to suggest hard
thoughts of God, and to beat off our souls from all
confidence in him, and expectations from him.   He
is the great causer of opposition between God and
the saints.   He reports the difficulties and fears
that are in our ways, with advantage, and labours
to weaken our hands, and discourage our hearts in
waiting upon God.   And these suggestions gain
the more credit with us, because they are confirmed and attested by sense and feeling.

But here is a desperate design, carrying on under very plausible pretences, against our souls.   It
concerns us to be watchful now, and maintain our
faith and hope in God.   How blessed is he who
can resign all to God, and quietly wait for his salvation!   To assist the soul in this difficulty, I shall
offer some further help, besides what hath been formerly given under the first creation, in the following considerations :

First consideration. Though Providence do not
yet perform the mercies you wait for, yet you have
no ground to entertain hard thoughts of God; for
it is possible God never gave you any ground for
your expectation of these things from him.   It
may be you have no promise to found your hope
upon ; and if so, why should God be suspected
and dishonoured by you in a case wherein his truth
and faithfulness were never engaged to you ? If we
are crossed in our outward concerns, and see our

expectations of prosperity dashed; if we see such or such an outward comfort removed, from which we promised ourselves much; why must God be accused for this? These things you promised yourselves; but where did God promise you prosperity, and the continuance of those comfortable things to you? Produce his promise, and show wherein he hath broken it. It is not enough for you to say, There are general promises in the Scripture, that " God will withhold no good thing," and these are good things which Providence withholds from you; for that promise, Psal. lxxxiv. 11, hath its limitations; it is expressly limited to such as " walk uprightly;" and it concerns you to examine whether you have done so, before you quarrel with Providence for non-performance of it. Ah! friend, search thine own heart, reflect upon thine own ways; seest thou not so many flaws in thine integrity, so many turnings aside from God, both in heart and life, that may justify God, not only in withholding what thou lookest for, but in removing all that thou enjoyest? And, besides this limitation as to the object, it is limited (as all other promises relating to externals are) in the matter or things promised, by the wisdom and will of God, which is the only rule by which they are measured out to men in this world; that is, such mercies, in such proportions as he sees needful and most conducive to your good; and these given out in such times and seasons as are of his own appointment, not yours.

God never came under an absolute, unlimited tie for outward comforts to any of us; and if we be disappointed, we can blame none but ourselves. Who bid us expect rest, ease, delight, and things of this kind in this world? He hath never told us,

18*

we shall be rich, healthy, and at ease in our habitations; but, on the contrary, he hath often told us
we must expect "troubles in the world," John
xvi. 33, and that "through many tribulations we
must enter into his kingdom," Acts xiv. 22. All
that he stands bound to us by promise for, is, to
"be with us in trouble," Psal. xci. 15, to supply
our real and absolute needs. "When the poor
and needy seek water, and there is none, and their
tongue faileth for thirst, I the Lord will hear them,
I the God of Israel will not forsake them," Isa.·
xli. 17, and to sanctify all these providences to our
good at last: "All things work together for
good to them that love God," Rom. viii. 28. And,
as to all these things, not one tittle ever did or shall
fail.

Second consideration. But if you say, you have
long waited upon God for spiritual mercies to your
souls, according to the promise, and still those
mercies are deferred, and your eyes fail whilst you
look for them; I would desire you seriously to
consider of what kind those spiritual mercies are,
for which you have so long waited upon God.
Spiritual mercies are of two sorts; such as belong
to the essence, the very being of the new creature,
without which it must fail; or, its well-being, and
the comfort of the inner man, without which you
cannot live so cheerfully as you would. The
mercies of the former kind are absolutely necessary, and therefore put into absolute promises, as
you read: "And I will make an everlasting covenant with them, that I will not turn away from
them to do them good, but I will put my fear in
their hearts, that they shall not depart from me,"
Jer. xxxii. 40. But for the rest, they are dispensed to us in such measures, and at such seasons

as the Lord sees fit, and many of his own people live for a long time without them. The donation and continuation of the Spirit to quicken, sanctify, and unite us with Christ, are necessary, but his joys and comforts are not so. A child of light may "walk in darkness," Isa. l. 10; he lives by faith, and not by feeling.

Third consideration. You complain, Providence delays to perform to you the mercies you have prayed and waited for; but have you right ends in your desires after these mercies? It may be that this is the cause you ask and receive not, James iv. 3. The want of a good aim is the reason why we want good success in our prayers. It may be we pray for prosperity, and our end is to please the flesh : we look no higher than the pleasure and accommodation of the flesh : we beg and wait for deliverance from such a trouble and affliction, not that we might be the more ready and prepared for obedience, but freed of what is grievous to us, and destroys our pleasure in the world. Certainly, if it be so, you have more need to judge and condemn yourselves, than to censure and suspect the care of God.

Fourth consideration. You wait for good, and it comes not; but is your will brought to a due submission to the will of God about it? Certainly God will have you come to this before you enjoy your desires. Enjoyment of your desires is the thing that will please you; but resignation of your wills is that which is pleasing to God. If your hearts cannot come to this, mercies cannot come to you. David was made to wait long for the mercies promised him, yea, and to be content without it, before he enjoyed it; he was brought to be "as a weaned child," Psal. cxxxi. 2, and so must you.

Fifth consideration. Your betters have waited long upon God for mercy, and why should not you? David waited till his "eyes failed," Psal. lxix. 3. The church "waited for him in the way of his judgments," Isa. xxvi. 8. Are you better than all the saints that are gone before you? Is God more obliged to you than to all his people? They have quietly waited, and why should not you?

Sixth consideration. Will you lose any thing by patiently waiting upon God for mercies? Certainly not at all; yea, it will turn to a double advantage to you to continue in a quiet, submissive, waiting posture upon God: for though you do not yet enjoy the good you wait for, yet all this while you are exercising your grace; and it is more excellent to act grace, than to enjoy comfort. All this while the Lord is training you up in the exercise of faith and patience, and bending your wills in submission to himself; and what do you lose by that? Yea, whenever the desired mercy comes, it will be so much the sweeter to you; for how much faith and prayer have been employed to produce it, how many wrestlings you have had with God for it; so many more degrees of sweetness you will find in it, when it comes. O, therefore, faint not, however long God delay you.

Seventh consideration. Are not these mercies you expect from God worth the waiting for? If not, it is your folly to be troubled for the want of them: if they be, why do not you continue waiting? Is it not all that God expects from you for the mercies he bestows upon you, that you wait upon him for them? You know you have not de-

served the least of them at his hands.   You expect
them not as a recompense, but a free favour ; and
if so, then certainly the least you can do is to wait
upon his pleasure for them.

Eighth consideration.   Consider how many promises are made in the word to waiting souls.   One
Scripture calls them " blessed that wait for him,"
Isa. xxx. 18.   Another tells us, " none that wait
for him shall be ashamed," Psal. xxv. 3, that is,
they shall not be finally disappointed, but at last
be partakers of their hopes.   A third scripture
tells us, " they that wait upon the Lord shall renew their strength," Isa. xl. 31, a promise you had
need make much use of in such a fainting time ;
with many more of like nature : and shall we faint
at this rate, in the midst of so many cordials as are
prepared to revive us in these promises ?

Ninth consideration.   How long hath God
waited upon you for the time when you will com-
ply with his commands, and come up to your engagements and promises ?   You have made God
wait long for your reformation and obedience, and
therefore have no reason to think it much if God
make you wait long for your consolation.   We
have our *how longs*, and hath not God his ?   We
cry, " But thou, O Lord, how long ?" Psal. vi. 3.
" How long wilt thou forget me, O Lord ? for
ever ?   How long wilt thou hide thy face from
me ?   How long shall I take counsel in my soul,
having sorrow in my heart daily ?   How long
shall mine enemy be exalted over me ?" Psal.
xiii. 1, 2.   But, surely, we should not think
these things long, when we consider how long
the Lord hath exercised his patience about us.
We have made him say, How long, how long ?
Our unbelief hath made him cry, " How long will

it be ere they believe me?" Numb. xiv. 11. Our corrupt hearts have made him cry, "How long shall vain thoughts lodge within thee?" Jer. iv. 14. Our impure natures and ways have made him cry, "How long will it be ere they attain to innocency?" Hosea viii. 5. If God wait upon you with so much patience for your duties, well may you wait upon him for his mercies.

Tenth consideration. This impatience and unbelief of yours, expressed in your weariness to wait any longer, as it is a great evil in itself, so, very probably, it is that evil which obstructs the way of your expected mercies; you might have your mercies sooner, if your spirits were quiet and more submissive. And thus of the second case.

The third case. How may a Christian discern when a providence is sanctified, aud comes from the love of God to him?

There are two sorts or kinds of providences concerning men in this world, the issues and events of which are vastly different, yea, contrary to each other. To some, all providences are overruled and ordered for good, according to that blessed promise, "And we know that all things work together for good to them that love God, to them who are the called according to his purpose," Rom. viii. 28, not only things that are good in themselves, as ordinances, graces, duties, and mercies; but things that are evil in themselves, as temptations, afflictions, and even their sins and corruptions, shall turn, in the issue, to their advantage and benefit. For though sin be so intrinsically and formally evil in its own nature, that, in itself, it be not capable of sanctification, yet, out of this worst of evils, God can work good to his people; and though he never makes sin the instrument of good, yet his providence may make it the occasion of good to his people, so that spiritual benefits may, by the wise overruling of Providence, be occasioned to the people of God by it. And so for afflictions of all kinds, the greatest and sorest of them, they do work, by the influence of Providence, a great deal of good to the saints, and that not only as the occasions, but as the instruments and means of it. "By this shall the iniquity of Jacob be purged," Isa. xxvii. 9, that is, by the instrumentality of this sanctified affliction.

To other persons nothing is sanctified, either as an instrument or occasion of any spiritual good; but as the worst things are ordered to the benefit of the saints, so the best things wicked men enjoy do them no good. Their prayers are turned into sin, Psal. cix. 7; the ordinances are the savour of death, 2 Cor. ii. 16; the grace of God turned into wantonness, Jude, ver. 4; Christ himself a rock of offence, 1 Pet. ii. 8; their table a snare; Psal. lxix. 22; their prosperity their ruin, Prov. i. 32. As persons are, so things work for good or evil. "To the pure all things are pure, but to them that are defiled and unbelieving is nothing pure," Tit. i. 15. Seeing, therefore, the events of Providence fall out so opposite to each other upon the godly and ungodly, every thing furthering the eternal good of the one, and the ruin of the other, it cannot but be acknowledged a most important case, in which every soul is deeply concerned, whether the providences under which he is, be sanctified to him or not.

For the clearing of which, I shall premise two necessary considerations, and then subjoin the rules which will be useful for the determination of the question.

1. Let it be considered, that we cannot know
from the matter of the things before us, whether
they be sanctified or unsanctified to us; for so considered, " All things come alike to all; and no man
knoweth either love or hatred by all the things that
are before him," Eccles. ix. 1, 2. We cannot understand the mind and heart of God by the things
he dispenseth with his hand. If prosperous providences befall us, we cannot say, Herein is a sure
sign that God loves me; for who hath more of
those providences than the people of his wrath ?
" They have more than their hearts can wish,
Psal. lxxiii. 7. Sure that must be a weak evidence
for heaven, which accompanies so great a part of
the world to hell.

By these things we may testify our love to God;
but, from ten thousand such enjoyments, we cannot get any solid assurance of his love to us.

And from these adverse, afflictive providences,
we cannot know God's hatred. If afflictions,
great afflictions, many afflictions, long-continued
afflictions, should set a brand, or fix a character of
God's hatred upon the persons on whom they fall,
where then shall we find God's people in the
world ? We must then seek out the proud, vain,
sensual wantons of the world, who spend their
days in pleasure, and say, These are the men whom
God loves.

Outward things are promiscuously dispensed,
and no man's spiritual estate is discernible by the
view of his temporal. When God draws the
sword, it may " cut off the righteous as well as the
wicked," Ezek. xxi. 3.

2. Though the providences of God materially
considered, afford no evidences of God's love to us,
yet the manner in which they befall us, and the

effects and fruits they produce in us, distinguish them very manifestly, and by them we may discern, whether they be sanctified providences, and fruits of the love of God, or not. But yet these effects and fruits of providences, by which we discern their nature, do not always presently appear; but time must be allowed for the soul's exercise under them. "Now no affliction for the present seemeth to be joyous, but grievous, nevertheless afterward it yieldeth the peaceable fruits of righteousness unto them which are exercised thereby," Heb. xii. 11.

The benefit of a providence is discerned as that of a medicine is; for the present it gripes, and makes the stomach sick and loathing, but afterwards we find the benefit of it, in our recovery of health and cheerfulness. Now, the providences of God being some of them comfortable, and others sad and grievous to nature, and the way to discern the sanctification and blessing of them being by the manner in which they come, and their operations upon our spirits, I shall consider the case as it respects both sorts of providences, and show you what effects of our troubles or comforts will speak them to be sanctified and blessed to us.

And, first, for sad and afflictive providences, in what kind or degree soever they befall us, we may warrantably conclude they are blessings to us, and come from the love of God, when,

(1.) They come in a proper season, when we have need of them, either to prevent some sin we are falling into, or recover us out of a remiss, supine, and careless frame of spirit, into which we are fallen. "If need be, ye are in heaviness," 1 Pet. i. 6. Certainly it is a good sign, that God designs your good by those troubles which are so

19

fitted and wisely ordered to suit the opportunity.
If you see the husbandman lopping a tree in the
proper season, it argues he aims at the fruitfulness
and flourishing of it; but, to do the same thing at
midsummer, speaks no regard to it, yea, his design
to destroy it.

(2.) When they are fitted both for quality and
degree, to work properly upon our predominant
corruptions, then they look like sanctified strokes.
The wisdom of God is much seen in the choice of
his rods. It is not any kind of trouble that will
work upon, and purge every sin; but, when God
sends such afflictions as, like medicine, are appro-
priated to the disease the soul labours under, this
speaks divine care and love. Thus, we may observe, it is usual with God to smite us in those
very comforts which stole away too much of the
love and delight of our souls from God; to cross
us in those things from which we raised up too
great expectations of comfort. These providences
speak the jealousy of God over us, and his care to
prevent far worse evils by these sad but needful
strokes. And so for the degrees of our troubles,
sanctified strokes are ordinarily fitted by the wisdom of God to the strength and ability of grace
within us. "In measure when it shooteth forth,
thou wilt debate with it; he stayeth his rough
wind in the day of the east wind," Isa. xxvii. 8.
It is an allusion to a physician, who exactly weighs
and measures all the ingredients which he mingles
in a potion for his sick patient, that it may be
proportionate to his strength, and no more; and so
much the next words intimate: "By this, therefore, shall the iniquity of Jacob be purged."

(3.) It is a good sign our troubles are sanctified
to us when they turn our hearts against sin, and

not against God. There are few great afflictions
which befall men that do not make them quarrel-
some and discontented. Wicked men quarrel with
God, and are filled with discontent against him.
So the Scripture describes them: "they were
scorched with great heat, and blasphemed the name
of God which hath power over these plagues,"
Rev. xvi. 9. But godly men, to whom afflictions
are sanctified, justify God, and fall out with sin,
they condemn themselves, and give glory to God.
" O Lord, righteousness belongeth unto thee, but
unto us confusion of faces," &c., Dan. ix. 7.
" Wherefore doth a living man complain, a man
for the punishment of his sins ?" Lam. iii. 39.
Happy afflictions, which make the soul fall out
and quarrel only with sin.

(4.) It is a sure sign afflicting providences are
sanctified when they purge the heart from sin, and
leave both heart and life more pure, heavenly,
mortified, and humble than they found them.
Sanctified afflictions are cleansers, they pull down
the pride, refine the earthliness, and purge out the
vanity of the spirit. So you read, Dan. xi. 35, it
purifies and makes their souls white. Hence it is
compared to a furnace, which separates the dross
from the pure metal. "Behold I have refined
thee, but not with silver; I have chosen thee in
the furnace of affliction," Isa. xlviii. 10. But, for
wicked men, let them be ever so long in the furnace, they lose no dross, Ezek. xxiv. 6. How
many Christians can bear witness to this truth !
After some sharp affliction hath been upon them,
how is the earthliness of their hearts purged.
They see no beauty, taste no more relish in the
world, than in the white of an egg. Oh, how serious, humble, and heavenly are they, till the im-

pressions made upon them by afflictions be worn
off and their deceitful lusts have again entangled
them! And this is the reason why we are so often
under the discipline of the rod. Let a Christian,
saith a late writer, be but two or three years without an affliction, and he is hardly good for any
thing; he cannot pray nor meditate, nor discourse
as he was wont to do; but, when a new affliction
comes, then he can find his tongue, and comes to
his knees again, and lives at another rate.

(5.) It is a good sign afflictive providences are
sanctified to us, when we draw near to God under
them, and "turn to him that smites us." A
wicked man under affliction "revolts more and
more," Isa. i. 5, "turns not to him that smites
him," Isa. ix. 13, but grows worse than before:
formality is turned into stupidity and indolence.

But if God afflict his own people with a sanctified rod, it awakens them to a more earnest seeking of God; it makes them pray more frequently,
spiritually, and fervently, than ever. When Paul
was buffeted by Satan, he "besought the Lord
thrice," 2 Cor. xii. 8.

(6.) We may conclude our afflictions to be sanctified, and to come from the love of God to us,
when they do not alienate our hearts from God,
but inflame our love to him. This is a sure rule;
whatever ends in the increase of our love to God,
proceeds from the love of God to us. A wicked
man finds his heart rising against God when he
smites him, but a gracious heart cleaves the closer
to him; he can love as well as justify an afflicting
God. "All this is come upon us; yet have we
not forgotten thee, neither have we dealt falsely in
thy covenant; our heart is not turned back, neither
have our steps declined from thy way; though

thou hast sore broken us in the place of dragons, and covered us with the shadow of death," Psal. xliv. 17—19. Here you have a true account of the temper and frame of a gracious soul under the greatest afflictions. To be "broken in the place of dragons, and covered with the shadow of death," imports the most dismal state of affliction; yet even then a gracious heart turns not back, that is, doth not for all this abate one drachm of love to God: God is as good and dear to him in afflictions as ever.

(7.) We may call our afflictions sanctified when divine teachings accompany them to our souls. "Blessed is the man whom thou chastenest, O Lord, and teachest him out of thy law," Psal. xciv. 12.   Sanctified afflictions are eye-salves; they teach us sensibly and effectually, when the Spirit accompanies them, the evil of sin, the vanity of the creature, the necessity of securing things that cannot be shaken.   Never doth a Christian take a truer measure both of his corruptions and graces than under the rod.   Now a man sees that filthiness which hath been long contracted in prosperity, what interest the creature hath in the heart, how little faith, patience, resignation and self-denial we can find, when God calls us to the exercise of them. O it is a blessed sign that trouble is sanctified, which makes a man thus turn in upon his own heart, search it, and humble himself before the Lord for the evils of it!

In the next place, let us take into consideration those other providences which are comfortable and pleasant. Sometimes they smile upon us in successes, prosperity, and the gratification of the desires of our hearts. Here the question will be, how the sanctification of these providences may be

19*

discovered to us. For resolution to this matter, I shall, for clearness' sake, lay down two sorts of rules; one negative, the other positive.

First, negative. 1. It is a sign that comfort is not sanctified to us which comes not, ordinarily, in the way of prayer. "The wicked boasteth of his heart's desire, and blesseth the covetous, whom the Lord abhorreth. The wicked, through the pride of his countenance, will not seek after God: God is not in all his thoughts," Psal. x. 3, 4. Here you see Providence may give men their hearts' desire, and yet they never once open their desires to God in prayer about it. But then those gifts of providence are only such as are bestowed on the worst of men, and are not the fruits of love.

2. Whatever success, prosperity, or comfort, men acquire by sinful mediums and indirect courses, are not sanctified mercies to them. This is not the method in which those mercies are bestowed. "Better is a little with righteousness, than great revenues without right," Prov. xvi. 8. Better upon this account that it comes in God's way, and with his blessing, which never follows the way of sin. God hath cursed the ways of sin, and no blessing can follow them.

3. Whatever prosperity or success makes men forget God, and cast off the care of duty, is not sanctified to them. It is unsanctified prosperity which lulls men asleep into a deep oblivion of God. "He made him ride on the high places of the earth, that he might eat the increase of the fields; and he made him to suck honey out of the rock, and oil out of the flinty rock, butter of kine, and milk of sheep, fat of lambs. and rams of the breed of Bashan, and goats, with the fat of kidneys of wheat, and thou didst drink the pure blood of the

grape ; but Jeshurun waxed fat and kicked ; thou
art waxen fat, thou art grown thick, thou art covered with fatness : then he forsook God which
made him, and lightly esteemed the rock of his salvation.   Of the rock that begat thee, thou art un-
mindful, and hast forgotten God that formed thee,"
Deut. xxxii. 13—18.   The rich are rarely grateful.

4. When prosperity is abused to sensuality, and
merely serves as fuel to maintain fleshly lusts, it is
not sanctified.   " They send forth their little ones
like a flock, and their children dance.   They take
the timbrel and harp, and rejoice at the sound of
the organ.   They spend their days in wealth, and
in a moment go down to the grave," Job xxi.
11—13.

5. It is a sign that prosperity is not sanctified to
men, when it swells the heart with pride and self-
conceit, like Nebuchadnezzar.   " At the end of
twelve months he walked in the palace of the kingdom of Babylon.   The king spake and said, Is not
this great Babylon that I have built for the house
of the kingdom, by the might of my power, and for
the honour of my majesty?" Dan. iv. 29, 30.

6. That success is not sanctified to men which
takes them off their duty, and makes them wholly
negligent, or very much indisposed to it.   " O generation, see ye the word of the Lord.   Have I been
a wilderness unto Israel?   A land of darkness?
Wherefore say my people, We are lords, we will
come no more unto thee?" Jer. ii. 31.

7. Nor can we think that prosperity sanctified
which wholly swallows up the souls of men in
their own enjoyments, and makes them regardless
of public miseries or sins.   " They lie upon beds
of ivory, and stretch themselves upon their couches,

and eat the lambs out of the flock, and the calves out of the midst of the stall. They chant to the sound of the viols, and invent to themselves instruments of music like David. They drink wine in bowls, and anoint themselves with the chief ointments; but they are not grieved for the affliction of Joseph," Amos vi. 4—6.

Second, positively. 1. Those mercies and comforts are undoubtedly sanctified to men, which humble their souls kindly before God, in the sense of their own vileness and unworthiness of them. Thus Jacob said, " I am not worthy of the least of all thy mercies," &c., Gen. xxxii. 10.

2. Sanctified mercies are commonly turned into cautions against sin, Ezra ix. 13, they are so many bands of restraint upon the soul that hath them to make them shun sin.

3. They will engage a man's heart in love to the God of his mercies; see Psal. xviii. 1, compared with the title.

4. They never satisfy a man as his portion, nor will the soul accept all the prosperity in the world, upon that score: like Moses, " esteeming the reproach of Christ greater riches than the treasures in Egypt: for he had respect unto the recompense of the reward," Heb. xi. 26.

5. Nor do they make men regardless of public sins or miseries; see Neh. ii. 1—3, compared with Acts vii. 23.

6. It is a sure sign that mercies are sanctified when they make the soul more ready and enlarged for God in duty. " Therefore the Lord established the kingdom in his hand, and all Judah brought to Jehoshaphat presents, and he had riches and honour in abundance, and his heart was lifted up in the ways of the Lord," &c., 2 Chron. xvii. 5, 6.

7. That which is obtained by prayer, and returned to God again in due praise, carries its own
testimonials with it, that it came from the love of
God, and is a sanctified mercy to the soul.   And
so much for this third case.

Fourth case. How may we attain unto an evenness and steadiness of spirit, under the changes
and contrary aspects of Providence upon us?

Three things are supposed in this case.

1. That Providence hath various and contrary
   aspects upon the people of God.

2. That it is a common thing with them to experience great disorders of spirit under those
   changes of Providence.

3. That these disorders may be, at least in a great
   measure, prevented by the due use and application of those rules and helps that God hath given
   us in such cases.

1. That Providence hath various, yea, contrary
aspects upon the people of God, is a case so plain,
that it needs no more than the mentioning, to let it
in to all our understandings.   Who of all the
people of God have not felt this truth? Providence
rings the changes all the world over: " He increaseth the nations, and destroyeth them; he en-
largeth the nations, and straiteneth them again,"
Job xii. 23.   The same it doth with persons:
" Thou hast lifted me up, and cast me down,"
Psal. cii. 10.   See what a sad alteration Providence
made upon the church: " How doth the city sit
solitary that was full of people!   How is she become as a widow!   She that was great among the
nations, and princess among the provinces, how
is she become tributary!   Is it nothing to you, all
ye that pass by? Behold and see if there be any
sorrow like unto my sorrow, which is done unto

me, wherewith the Lord hath afflicted me in the
day of his fierce anger," Lam. i. 1. 12. And how
great an instance was Job of this truth! See Job
xxix, compared with chap. xxx. How many
thousands have complained with Naomi, whose
condition hath been so strongly altered that others
have said, as the people of Bethlehemdid of her,
" Is this Naomi," Ruth i. 19—21.

2. These vicissitudes of Providence commonly
cause great disorders of spirit in the best of men. As
intense heat and cold try the strength and soundness of the constitution of our bodies, so the alterations made by Providence upon our conditions try
the strength of our graces, and too often discover
the weakness and corruption of holy men. Hezekiah was a good man; but yet his weakness and
corruption was discovered by the alterations Providence made upon his condition. When sickness and pains summoned him to the grave, what
bitter complaints and despondencies are recorded!
See Isa. xxxviii. And when Providence lifted him
up again into a prosperous condition, what osten-
tation and vain-glory did he discover! Isa. xxxix
2. David had more than a common stock of in-
herent grace, yet not enough to keep him in an
equal temper of spirit under great alterations. In
my prosperity, I said, I shall never be moved;
thou didst hide thy face, and I was troubled, Psal.
xxx. 6, 7. It is not every man that can say with
Paul, " I know both how to be abased, and I know
how to abound; every where, and in all things I
am instructed both to be full and to be hungry, both
to abound and to suffer need," Phil. iv. 12. He is
truly rich in grace, whose riches or poverty neither
hinders the acting nor impoverishes the stock of his
graces.

Though the best men be subject to such disorders of heart under the changes of Providence, yet these disorders may, in a great measure, be prevented by the due application of such rules and helps as God hath given us in such cases.

Now these helps are suited to a threefold aspect of providence upon us, namely, 1. Comfortable—2. Calamitous—3. Doubtful; to all which I shall speak particularly and briefly.

Question 1. How may we attain to an evenness and steadiness of heart under the comfortable aspects of Providence upon us?

Under providences of this kind, the great danger is, lest the heart be lifted up with pride and vanity, and fall into a drowsy and remiss temper. To prevent this, we had need to urge humbling and awakening considerations upon our heart; such are these that follow.

(1.) These gifts of Providence are common to the worst of men, and are no special distinguishing fruits of God's love. The vilest of men have been filled even to satiety with these things. "Their eyes stand out with fatness; they have more than heart could wish," Psal. lxxiii. 7.

(2.) Think how unstable and changeable all these things are. What you glory in to-day may be none of yours to-morrow. " Riches make themselves wings, and flee away, as an eagle towards heaven," Prov. xxiii. 5. As the wings of a fowl grow out of the substance of the body, so the cause of the creature's transitoriness is in itself; it is subjected to vanity, and that vanity, like wings, carries it away. They are but fading flowers, James i. 10.

(3.) The changes of providences are never nearer

to the people of God, than when their hearts are
lifted up or grown secure by prosperity. Doth
Hezekiah glory in his treasures? The next news
he hears is of an impoverishing providence at hand,
Isa. xxxix. 2—7. Others may be left to perish in
unsanctified prosperity, but you shall not.

(4.) This is a great discovery of the carnality
and corruption that is in thy heart: it argues a
heart little set on God, little mortified to the world,
little acquainted with the vanity and ensnaring nature of these things. O, you know not what hearts
you have till such providences try them; and is
not such a discovery matter of deep humiliation?

(5.) Was it not better with you in a low condition than it is now? Reflect, and compare state
with state, and time with time. How is the frame
of your hearts altered with the alteration of your
condition! So God complains of Israel: "I did
know thee in the wilderness—the land of drought.
According to their pasture, so were they filled;
they were filled, and their heart was exalted, therefore have they forgotten me," saith the Lord, Hos.
xiii. 5, 6: as if he had said, You and I were better acquainted formerly, when you were in a low
condition; prosperity hath estranged you, and altered the case. How sad is it, that God's mercies
should be the occasion of our estrangement from
him!

Question 2. Upon the other side, it is worth
considering, how our hearts may be established
and kept steady under calamitous and adverse providences.

Here we are in equal danger of the other extreme—despondency and sinking under the frowns
and strokes of cross providences. Now to sup-

port and establish the heart in this case take three helps.

(1.) Consider, that afflictive providences are of great use to the people of God; they cannot live without them. The earth doth not more need chastening frosts and mellowing snows, than our hearts do nipping providences. Let the best Christian be but for a few years without them, and he will be sensible of the want of them; he will find a sad remission and declining of all his graces.

(2.) No stroke or calamity upon the people of God can separate them from Christ: "Who shall separate us from the love of Christ? shall tribulation?" Rom. viii. 25. There was a time when Job could call nothing in this world but trouble his own: he could not say, my estate, my honour, my health, my children; for all these were gone; yet then he could say, "my Redeemer," Job xix. 25. Well, then, there is no cause to sink whilst interest in Christ remains sure to us.

(3.) All your calamities will have an end shortly. The longest day of the saints' troubles has an end, and then no more troubles for ever. The troubles of the wicked will be to eternity; but you shall "suffer but awhile," 1 Pet. v. 13. If a thousand troubles be appointed for you, they will come to one at last, and after that no more: yea, and though our troubles "be but a moment, yet they work for us a far more exceeding and eternal weight of glory," 2 Cor. iv. 1. Let that support your hearts under all your sufferings.

Question 3. Let us consider what may be useful to support and quiet our hearts under doubtful providences, when our dear concerns hang in a doubtful suspense before us, and we know not

20

which way the providence of God will cast and
determine them.

Now the best hearts are apt to grow solicitous
and pensive, distracted with thoughfulness, about
the event and issue. To relieve and settle us in
this case, the following considerations are very
useful.

(1.) Let us consider the vanity and inutility of
such a solicitude: "Which of you," saith our
Lord, "by taking thought can add one cubit unto
his stature?" Matt. vi. 27. We may break our
peace, and waste our spirits, but not alter the case.
We cannot turn God out of his way: "He is in
one mind," Job xxiii. 13. We may, by struggling
against God increase, but not avoid, or lighten our
troubles.

(2.) How often do we afflict and torment ourselves by our own unquiet thoughts, when there
is no real cause or ground for so doing! "Thou
hast feared continually every day, because of the
fury of the oppressor, as if he were ready to destroy; and where is the fury of the oppressor?"
Isa. li. 13. Oh what abundance of disquiet and
trouble might we prevent, by waiting quietly till
we see the issues of providence, and not bringing,
as we do, the evils of the morrow upon the day!

(3.) What a great ground of quietness is it, that
the whole disposal and management of all our affairs and concerns is in the hand of our own God
and Father! No creature can touch us without
his commission or permission. "I know," saith
Christ, "thou couldst have no power against me,
except it were given thee from above," John xix.
11. Neither men nor devils can act any thing
without God's leave; and be sure he will sign no
order to your prejudice.

(4.) What a great satisfaction must it be to all that believe the Divine authority of the Scriptures, that the faithfulness of God stands engaged for every line and syllable found therein! And how many blessed lines in the Bible may we mark that respect even our outward concerns, and the happy issue of them all! Upon these two grounds, that our outward concerns, with their steady direction to a blessed end, are found in the word; and this word being of Divine authority, the faithfulness and honour of God stands good for every tittle that is found there; I say, upon these grounds is such stability, that our minds may repose with the greatest security and confidence upon them, even in the cloudiest day of trouble. Not only your eternal salvation, but your temporal interests are there secured. Be quieted, therefore, in the confidence of a blessed issue.

(5.) How great and sure an expedient have the saints ever found it to their own peace, to commit all doubtful issues of providence to the Lord, and devolve all their cares upon him! "Commit thy works unto the Lord, and thy thoughts shall be established," Prov. xvi. 3. By works he means any doubtful, intricate, perplexing business, about which our thoughts are racked and tortured. Roll all these upon the Lord by faith, leave them with him, and the present, immediate benefit you shall have by it, (besides the comfort in the last issue) shall be tranquillity and peace in your thoughts! And who is there of any standing or experience in religion that hath not found it so?

Fifth case. How may a Christian work his heart into a resigned frame to the will of God, when sad providences approach him, and presage great troubles and afflictions coming on towards him?

For the right stating and resolving of this important case it will be needful to show, 1. What is not included and intended in the question; 2. What it doth suppose and include in it; and, 3. What helps and directions are necessary for the due performance of this great and difficult duty.

1. Negatively. It must be premised, that the question doth not suppose the heart or will of a Christian to be at his own command and disposal in this matter; we cannot resign it and subject it to the will of God whenever we desire so to do. The duty indeed is ours, but the power by which alone we perform it is God's: we act as we are actuated by the Spirit. It is with our hearts, as with meteors hanging in the air by the influence of the sun; while that continues, they abide above; but when it fails, they fall to the earth. We can do this, and all things else, be they ever so difficult, "through Christ that strengthens us," Phil. iv. 13; "but without him we can do nothing," John xv. 5. He doth not say, Without me ye can do but little; or, Without me ye can do nothing, but with great difficulty; or, Without me ye can do nothing perfectly; but, Without me ye can do nothing at all. And every Christian hath a witness in his own breast to attest this truth; for there are cases frequently occurring in the methods of Providence, in which, notwithstanding all their prayers and desires, all their reasonings and strivings, they cannot quiet their hearts fully in the disposal and will of God; but, on the contrary, they find all their endeavours in this matter to be but as the rolling of a returning stone against the hill. Till God

say to the heart, Be still; and to the will, Give up, nothing can be done.

2. Affirmatively. Let us consider what this case doth suppose and include in it, and we shall find.

[1.] That it supposes the people of God to have a foresight of troubles and distresses approaching and drawing near to them. I confess it is not always so, for many of our afflictions, as well as comforts, come by way of surprises upon us; but oftentimes we have forewarnings of troubles both public and personal, before we feel them: as the weather may be discerned by the face of the sky. When we see a morning sky red and lowering, this is a natural sign of a foul and rainy day, Matt. xvi. 3. And there are as certain signs of the times whereby we may discern when trouble is near, even at the door; and these forewarnings are given by the Lord to awaken us to our duties, by which they may either be prevented, Zeph. ii. 1, 2, or sanctified and sweetened to us when they come. These signs and notices of approaching troubles are gathered, partly from the observation and collation of parallel Scripture cases and examples, God generally holding one tenor and steady course in the administration of his providences in all ages, 1 Cor. x. 6; partly from the reflections Christians make upon the frames and tempers of their own hearts, which greatly need awakening, humbling, and purging providences; for let a Christian be but a few years or months without a rod, and how formal, earthly, dead, and vain will his heart grow! And such a temper presages affliction to them that are beloved of the Lord. Lastly, The ordering and disposing of the next causes into a posture and

20 *

preparation for our trouble, plainly premonishes us, that trouble is at the door. Thus, when the symptoms of sickness begin to appear upon our own bodies, the wife of our bosom, or our children, (which are as our own souls,) Providence herein awakens our expectations of death and doleful separations: so when enemies combine together, and plot the ruin of our liberties, estates, or lives, and God seems to loose the bridle of restraint upon their necks, now we cannot but be alarmed with the near approach of troubles, especially when, at the same time, our consciences reflect upon the abuse and non-improvement of these our threatened comforts.

[2.] The case before us supposes that these premonitions and forerunners of affliction do usually very much disturb the order, and break the peace of our souls; they put the mind under great discomposure, the thoughts under much distraction, and the affections into tumults and rebellion.

Ah! how unwilling are we to surrender to the Lord the loan which he lent us! to be disquieted by troubles, when at ease in our enjoyments! How unwelcome are the messengers of affliction to the best of men! We are ready to say to them as the widow to Elijah, "What have I to do with thee, O thou man (O messenger) of God? art thou come unto me to call my sin to remembrance, and to slay my son?" 1 Kings xvii. 18. And this ariseth partly from the remains of corruption in the best souls; for though every sanctified person is come by his own consent into the kingdom, and under the government and sceptre of Christ, and every thought of his heart must of right be subjected to him 2 Cor. x. 5, yet the conquest and power of

grace is but incomplete, and in part; and natural
corruption, like Jeroboam with his vain men, riseth
up, against it, and causeth many mutinies in the
soul, whilst grace, like young Abijah, is weak-
handed, and cannot resist them; and partly from
the advantage Satan makes of the season to irritate
and assist our corruptions: he knows that what
is already in motion is the more easily moved.
In this confusion and hurry of thoughts he undis-
cernedly shuffles in his temptations; sometimes
aggravating the evils which we fear, with all the
sinking and overwhelming circumstances imagina-
ble; sometimes divining and forecasting such events
and evils, as, haply, never fall out; sometimes
repining at the disposals of God, as more severe to
us than to others; and sometimes reflecting with
very unbelieving and unworthy thoughts upon the
promises of God, and his faithfulness in them; by
all which the affliction is made to sink deep into
the soul before it actually comes; the thoughts are
so disordered, that duty cannot be duly performed;
and the soul is really weakened and disabled to
bear its trial when it comes indeed: just as if a
man should be kept waking and restless all the
night with the thoughts of his hard journey which
he must travel to-morrow; and so when to-morrow
is come, he faints for want of rest, midway on his
journey.

[3.] It is here supposed to be the Christian's
great duty, under the apprehensions of approaching troubles, to resign his will to God's, and quietly
commit the events and issues of all to him, whatever they may prove. Thus did David in the like
case and circumstances: "And the king said unto
Zadok, Carry back the ark of God into the city.

If I shall find favour in the eyes of the Lord, he will bring me back again, and show me both it and his habitation : but if he thus say, I have no delight in thee, behold here am I, let him do to me as seemeth good unto him," 2 Sam. xv. 25, 26.

Oh, lovely and truly Christian temper! As if he had said, Go, Zadok, return with the ark to its place : though I have not the symbol, yet I hope I shall have the real presence of God with me in this sad journey : how he will dispose the events of this sad and doubtful providence, I know not ; either I shall return again to Jerusalem, or I shall not : if I do, then I shall see it again, and enjoy the Lord in his ordinances there : if I do not, then I shall go to that place where there is no need or use of those things ; and either way it will be well for me. I am content to refer all to the Divine pleasure, and commit the issue, be it whatever it will, to the Lord.

Till our hearts come to the like resolve, we can have no peace within. "Commit thy works unto the Lord, and thy thoughts shall be established," Prov. xvi. 3. By works he means not only every enterprise and business we undertake, but every puzzling, intricate, and doubtful event we fear. These being once committed by an act of faith, and our wills resigned unto his, besides the comfort we shall have in the issue, we shall have the present advantage of a well composed and peaceful spirit.

But this resignation is the difficulty. No doubt of peace, could we once bring our hearts to that. And therefore,

[4.] I shall here subjoin such helps and directions, as may, through God's blessing, in the faithful use of them, assist and facilitate this great and difficult work.

First help. Labour to work into your hearts a deep and fixed sense of the infinite wisdom of God, and your own folly and ignorance. This will make resignation easy to you. Whatsoever the Lord doth is by counsel, Eph. i. 11, his understanding is infinite, Psal. cxlvii. 5, his thoughts are very deep, Psal. xcii. 5, but, as for man, yea, the wisest among men, how little doth his understanding penetrate the works and designs of Providence! And how often are we forced to retract our rash opinions, and confess our mistakes; acknowledging, that if Providence had not seen with better eyes than ours, and looked further than we did, we had precipitated ourselves into a thousand mischiefs, which, by its wisdom and care, we have escaped. It is well for us that the seven eyes of Providence are ever awake, and looking out for our good. Now, if one creature can and ought to be guided and governed by another that is more wise and skilful than himself, as the client by his learned counsel, the patient by his skilful physician, much more should every creature give up his weak reason, and shallow understanding, to the infinite wisdom of the omniscient God.

It is nothing but our pride and arrogance, over-ruling our understandings, that makes resignation so hard. Carnal reason seems to itself a wise disputant about the concerns of the flesh, but how often hath Providence baffled it. The more humility, the more resignation.

How few of our mercies and comforts have been foreseen by us! Our own projects have come to nothing, and that which we never thought on, or contrived, hath taken place. Not our choice of the ground, nor skill in weighing and delivering the bowl, but some unforeseen providence, like a rub in the green, was that which made the cast.

Second help. Deeply consider the sinfulness and vanity of torturing your own thoughts about the issues of doubtful providences.

1. There is much sin in so doing: for all our anxious and solicitous emotions, what else are they than the immediate issues and fruits of pride and unbelief?

There is not a greater discovery of pride in the world than in the contests of our wills with the will of God. It is a presumptuous invading of God's prerogative to dictate to his providence, and prescribe to his wisdom.

2. There is a great deal of vanity in it: all the thoughtfulness in the world will not make one hair white or black; all our discontents will not prevail with God to call back, or (as the word may be rendered,) make void his word, Isa. xxxi. 2. He is in one mind, Job xxiii. 13. The thoughts of his mind are from everlasting, Psal. xxxiii. 11.

Third help. Set before you those choice Scripture patterns of submission to the Lord's will, in as deep, yea, much deeper points of self-denial than this before you, and shame yourselves out of this quarrelling temper with Providence.

You know what a close trial that providence was to Abraham, that called him from his native country and father's house, to go he knew not whither; and yet it is said in Isaiah xli. 2, " He came to God's foot," as readily obeying his call, as a servant when his master knocks for him with his foot.

Paul's voyage to Jerusalem had a dismal aspect upon himself; he could expect nothing but bonds and afflictions as he tells us, Acts xx. 23. And a great trial it was to the saints, who could not tell how to give up such a minister, yet he resigns up his will to God's, and so do they, Acts xxi. 14, " The will of the Lord be done."

But far beyond these, and all other patterns, what an example hath our dear Lord Jesus set before us in the deepest point of self-denial that ever was in the world, when the Father gave the cup of suffering into his hand in the garden, Mark xiv. 36, a cup of wrath, the wrath of the great and terrible God, and that without mixture ; the very taste whereof put nature into an agony and astonishment, a sore amazement, a bloody sweat, and forced from him that vehement and sad cry, " Father, if it be possible, let this cup pass ;" yet still, with submission, " nevertheless, not my will, but thine be done." Oh, blessed pattern of obedience and resignation to the pleasure of God ! What is your case to this?

Fourth help. Study the singular benefits and advantages of a will resigned to, and melted into the will of God.

1. Such a spirit hath a continual sabbath within itself: the thoughts are established, Prov. xvi. 3. And truly, till a man come to this he doth but too much resemble the devil, who is a restless spirit, seeking rest but finding none.

It was an excellent expression of Luther, to one that was much perplexed in his spirit about the doubtful events of some affairs of his that were then pending : " The Lord shall do all for thee, and thou shalt do nothing, but be the Sabbath of Christ."

It is by this means that the Lord gives his beloved
sleep, Psal. cxxvii. 2.   He means not the sleep of
the body, but of the spirit.   Though believers live
in the midst of many troubles here, yet with quiet
and composed minds they keep themselves in the
silence of faith, as though they were asleep.

2. Besides, it fits a man's spirit for communion
with God in all his afflictions, and this alleviates
and sweetens them beyond any thing in the world.

3. And surely a man is never nearer the mercy
he desires, or the deliverance he expects, (as one
truly observes,) than when his soul is brought into
a submissive temper.   David was never nearer the
kingdom than when he became as a weaned child.

Fifth help. Lastly, think how repugnant an un-
submissive temper is, both to your prayers and
professions.   You pray that the will of God may
be done on earth as it is in heaven, and yet, when
it seems to cross your wills or interests, you strug-
gle and fret against it.   You profess to have committed your souls to his keeping, and to leave your
eternal concerns in his hands; and yet cannot
commit things, infinitely less valuable, unto him.
How contradictory are these things!

Your profession, as Christians, speaks you to be
led by the Spirit; but this practice speaks you to
follow the perverse counsels of your own spirits.
O then regret no more, dispute no more, but lie
down meekly at your Father's feet, and say, in all
cases, and at all times, the will of the Lord be
done.

And thus I have, through the aid of Providence,
performed what I designed to speak from this
Scripture.   I acknowledge my performances have
been accompanied with much weakness, yet I have

endeavoured to speak of Providence the things that are right.   Blessed be the Lord, who hath thus far assisted and protected me in this work.

How Providence will dispose of my life, liberty, and labours, for the time to come, I know not; but I cheerfully commit all to him who hath "performed all things for me."

POSTSCRIPT.

In consideration of the great and manifold advantages resulting from a humble and heedful observation of Providence, I cannot but judge it the con-
cernment of Christians, who have time and ability
for such a work, to keep written memorials or jour-
nals of providences by them, for their own and
others' use and benefit. For want of collecting
and communicating such observations, not only
ourselves, but the church of God suffers loss and
is impoverished.

Some say the art of medicine was thus acquired
and perfected. When any one had met with some
rare medicinal herb, and accidentally discovered
the virtues of it, he would post it up in some public place; and so the physician attained his skill
by a collection of those posted experiments and
receipts.

I am not for posting up all that a Christian knows
or meets with in his experience; for, as I have
said before, religion doth not lay all open; but yet
there is a prudent, humble, and seasonable com-
munication of our experiences and observations of
Providence, which is exceedingly beneficial both
to ourselves and our brethren.

If Christians, in reading the Scriptures, would
judiciously collect and record the providences they
meet with there; and, if destitute of other helps,
they would but add those that have fallen out in
their own time and experience, Oh what a precious treasure would these make! How would it
prove an antidote to their souls against the spread-

ing atheism of these days, and satisfy them, beyond what many other arguments can do, that " The Lord he is God, the Lord he is God."

While this work was under my hand, I was both delighted and assisted by a pious and useful essay of an unknown author, (Mr. T. C. in his Isagoge,) who hath, to very good purpose, improved many scriptural passages of providence, which seem to lie out of the road of common observation; some passages I have noted out of it, which have been sweet to me. O that Christians would every where set themselves to such work! Providence carries our lives, liberties, and concerns in God's hand every moment. Your bread is in his cupboard, your money in his purse, your safety in his enfolding arms; and sure it is the least part of what you owe, to record the favours you receive at his hands. More particularly,

1. Trust not your slippery memories with such a multitude of remarkable passages of providence as you have met, and shall meet with in your way to heaven. It is true, things that greatly affect us are not easily forgotten by us; and yet, how common is it for new impressions to erase our former ones. It was a saying of that worthy man, Dr. Harris, " My memory never failed me in all my life; for indeed, I durst never trust it." Written memorials secure us against that hazard; and besides, make them useful to others when we are gone; so that you carry not away all your treasure to heaven with you, but leave these choice legacies to your surviving friends. Certainly it were not so great a loss to lose your silver, your goods and chattels, as it is to lose your experiences which God hath this way given you in this world.

2. Take heed of clasping up those rich treasures

in a book, and thinking it enough to have noted
them there; but have frequent recourse to them as
often as new wants, fears, or difficulties arise and
assault you.   Now it is seasonable to consider and
reflect, Was I never so distressed before? Is this
the first plunge that ever befell me? "Let me consider the days of old, the years of ancient times,"
as Asaph did, Psal. lxxvii. 5.

3. Beware of slighting former straits and dangers, in comparison with present ones.   That
which is next us, always appears greatest to us:
and as time removes us further and further from our
former mercies or dangers, so they lessen in our
eyes, just as the land from which they sail, doth
to seamen.   Know that your dangers have been
as great, and your fears no less formerly than now.
Make it as much your business to preserve the
sense and value, as the memory of former providences, and the fruit will be sweet to you.

EXTRACTS FROM THE LAST CHAPTER OF THE RIGHTEOUS MAN'S REFUGE.

THE AGGRAVATIONS OF A WICKED MAN'S TROUBLES.

1. When troubles come upon him, the curse of God follows him into his carnal refuges; "Cursed be the man that trusteth in man, and maketh flesh his arm, and whose heart departeth from the Lord," Jer. xvii. 5. Trouble is the arrow, and this curse the venom of the arrow, which makes the wound incurable.

2. When troubles fall upon him from without, a guilty conscience will terrify him from within; so that the mind can give no relief to the body, but both sink under their own weights. It is not so with the people of God. They have inward relief under outward pressures, 2 Cor. iv. 16.

3. The gusts and storms of wicked men's troubles may blow them into hell, and hurry them into eternal destruction: if death march towards them upon the pale horse, hell always follows him, Rev. vi. 8.

4. If troubles and distresses overwhelm their hearts, they can give them no vent or ease by prayer, faith, and resignation to God, as his people use to do.

5. When their troubles and distresses come, then come the hour and power of their temptations; and, to shun sorrow, they will fall into sin, having no promise to be kept in the hour of temptation, as the saints have, Rev. iii. 10.

6. When their troubles come, they will be left alone in the midst of them: these are their burdens, and they alone must bear them. God's gracious, comfortable, supporting presence is only with his own people.

7. If trouble and death come upon them as a storm, they have no anchor of hope to drop in the storm; "The wicked is driven away in his wickedness; but the righteous hath hope in his death," Prov. xiv. 32. By all which it appears that a Christless person is a most helpless and shiftless creature in the day of trouble.

REASONS WHY CHRISTIANS SHOULD NOT BE DEJECTED.

1. If thou be in Christ, thy sins are forgiven thee; and why should not a pardoned soul be a cheerful soul in adversity? Afflictions may buzz and hum about thee, like bees that have lost their sting, but they can never hurt thee.

2. If thou be in Christ, thy God is with thee in all thy troubles; and how can thy heart sink or faint in such a presence? Let those who are alone in troubles fail under them: but do not thou do so, who art surrounded with Almighty power, grace, and love, Isa. xliii. 1, 2.

3. If thou be in Christ, thy greatest afflictions shall prove thy best friends and benefactors, Rom. viii. 28. Surely then thou art more afraid than hurt; thou mistakest thy best friends for thy worst enemies; thou and thy afflictions shall part more comfortably than you met.

4. If thou be in Christ, thy treasure is safe, thy eternal happiness is out of the reach of all thine enemies, Luke xii. 4; x. 42: and if that be safe, thou hast no cause to be sad. To droop and tremble at the hazard of earthly comforts, whilst heaven-

ly and eternal things are safe, is as if a man that had obtained his pardon from the king, and had it safe in his bosom, should be found weeping upon the way home, because he hath lost his staff or glove. These reasons are strong against the dejections of God's people under outward troubles; but yet I am sensible that all the reasoning in the world will not prevent their dejections, except they will take pains to clear up their interest in God against such a day, Psal. xviii. 2, and will act their faith by way of adherence and dependence upon God, in the want of former light and evidence, Isa. l. 10. And lastly, that they keep their consciences pure and inviolate, which will be a spring of comfort in the midst of troubles, 2 Cor. i. 12.

CHRISTIAN RESIGNATION.

There are six things implied in Christian resignation.

1. An awakened sense of our dangers and hazards. "At what time I am afraid, I will trust in thee," Psal. lvi. 3. Suffering times are resigning times; "Let them that suffer according to the will of God commit the keeping of their souls to him in well doing, as unto a faithful Creator," 1 Pet. iv. 19. And the greater and nearer our dangers are, the more frequent and vigorous should the actings of our faith this way be: Be not far from me, for trouble is near.

2. Resignation to God necessarily implies our renunciation and disclaiming of all other refuges. "Asshur shall not save us, we will not ride upon horses, neither will we say any more to the work of our hands, Ye are our gods, for in thee the fatherless findeth mercy," Hos. xiv. 3. He that relies upon God must cease from man; resignation

to God excludes not the use of lawful means, but
it doth exclude dependence upon them.

3. Resignation to God is always grounded upon
an interest in God. We have no warrant nor encouragement to expect protection from him in time
of trouble, except we can come to him as children
to a father; it is the filial relation that gives encouragement to this fiducial resignation; and the
clearer that relation and interest is, the more bold
and confident those acts of faith will be; "Preserve my soul, for I am holy : O thou, my God,
save thy servant that trusteth in thee," Psal. lxxxvi.
2. And again, "I am thine, save me," Psal. cxix.
94. I speak not here of the first act of faith which
flows not from an interest, but gives the soul an
interest in God. Nor do I say, that poor, doubting and timorous believers, whose interest in him
is dark and dubious, have no warrant to resign
themselves and their concerns into his hands; for
it is both their right and duty to do it : but certainly
the clearer our interest is, the more easy and comfortable will those acts be.

4. The committing acts of faith imply a full acknowledgment and owning of God's power to protect us, be the danger ever so imminent; "My
times are in thy hand, deliver me from the hands
of mine enemies, and from them that persecute me,"
Psal. xxxi. 15. This denotes, O Lord, I am fully
satisfied, my life is not at the disposal of mine
enemies; it is not in their hands, but in thine; all
the traps and snares they lay for it shall not shorten
one minute of my time. I know thy hand is fully
able to protect me, and therefore into thy hands I
resign myself, and all I have.

5. Resignation involves in it an expectation of
help and safety from God, when we see no way of

security from men, "O Lord," saith Jehoshaphat, "we have no might, nor strength, neither know we what to do, but our eyes are unto thee," 2 Chron. xx. 12. So David, "My soul, wait thou only upon God; for my expectation is from him: he only is my rock and my salvation; he is my defence; I shall not be moved," Psal. lxii. 5, 6.

6. Resignation to God implies the leaving of ourselves, and our concerns with him, to be disposed of according to his good pleasure; the resigning soul desires the Lord to do with him what he will, and is content to take what lot divine pleasure shall cast for him: "And the king said unto Zadok, Carry back the ark of God into the city; if I shall find favour in the eyes of the Lord, he will bring me again, and show me both it and his habitation; but if he thus say, I have no delight in thee, behold, here am I, let him do to me as seemeth good unto him," 2 Sam. xv. 25.

ENCOURAGEMENTS TO TRUST IN GOD.

1. The sovereignty and absolute dominion of God over all creatures is a singular encouragement to commit ourselves into his hands, and trust him above all. "Because of his strength will I wait upon thee: for God is my defence," Psal. lix. 9. If a man were in danger amidst a great army of rude and insolent soldiers, and were to put himself under the protection of any one, it would be his wisdom to choose to do it under the general, who had all the soldiers of his army at his beck. Christian, thy God, into whose hands thou committest thyself, is Lord-General of all the hosts and armies in heaven and earth; how safe art thou then in his hands!

2. The unsearchable and perfect wisdom of God
is a mighty encouragement to commit ourselves
into his hands; "With him is plenteous redemp-
tion," Psal. cxxx. 7, 8, that is, choice and variety
of ways and methods to save his people. We are,
but God never is, at a loss to find a door for our
escape. "The Lord knoweth how to deliver the
godly out of temptation," 2 Pet. ii. 9.

3. The infinite tenderness and compassion of our
God, is a sweet encouragement to resign and commit ourselves and all we have into his hands; his
mercy is incomparably tender towards his people,
infinitely beyond whatever any creature felt stirring
within towards his own most beloved child, Isa.
xlix. 15. This compassion of God engageth the
two fore-mentioned attributes, namely, his power
and wisdom, for the preservation and relief of his
people, as often as distresses befall them. Yea,

4. The very distresses his people are in do, as
it were, awake the Almighty power of God for
their defence and rescue; our distresses are not
only proper seasons, but powerful motives to his
saving power. "For the Lord shall judge his people,
and repent himself for his servants when he seeth
that their power is gone, and there is none shut up
or left," Deut. xxxii. 36. God makes it an argument to himself, and his people plead it as an argument with him, "Be not far from me, for trouble
is near, for there is none to help."

5. We have already committed greater and
weightier concernments into his hand than the
dearest interest we have in this world; we have
entrusted our souls with him, 1 Pet. iv. 19; 2 Tim.
i. 12. Well, therefore, may we commit the lesser,
who have entrusted the greater with him. What
are our lives, liberties, estates, and relations, com-

pared with our souls, and the eternal safety and
happiness of them!

6. The committing act of faith is the great and
only expedient to procure and secure the peace
and tranquillity of our minds, amidst all the distractions and troubles of the present world. The
greatest part of our affliction and trouble in such
days is from the working of our own thoughts;
these torments from within are worse than any
from without; and the resignation of all to God by
faith is their best and only cure. "Commit thy
works unto the Lord, and thy thoughts shall be
established," Prov. xvi. 3. A blessed calmness
of mind, a sweet tranquillity and settlement of
thoughts follow immediately hereupon, Psal. cxiv.
19. O then leave all with God, and quietly expect
a comfortable issue: and for the better settlement
and security of thy peace in times of distraction
and trouble, I beseech thee, reader, carefully to
watch and guard against these two evils:

Caution 1. Beware of infidelity or distrustful-
ness of God and his promises, which secretly
lurks in thy heart, and is very apt to betray itself
when great distresses and troubles befall thee.
Thou wilt know it by such symptoms as these:
1. In an over-hasty and eager desire after present
deliverance; "The captive exile hasteneth that he
may be loosed, and that he should not die in the
pit, nor that his bread should fail," Isa. li. 14.
The less faith, always the more impatience; and
the more ability to believe, the more patience to
wait. 2. It will discover itself in our readiness to
close with, and catch at sinful mediums and methods of deliverance, Isa. xxx. 15, 16. And this
is the handle of temptation, and occasion of apostasy. "But he that believeth will not make haste,"

Isa. xxviii. 16. No more haste than good speed. 3. It will show itself in distracting cares and fears about events which will rack the mind with various and endless tortures.

Caution 2. Beware of dejection and despondency of mind in evil times; take heed of a poor low spirit that will presently sink and give up its hope upon every appearance and face of trouble; it is a promise made unto the righteous, " He shall not be afraid of evil tidings, his heart is fixed, trusting in the Lord," Psal. cxii. 7. The trusting of God fixes the heart, and the fixing of the heart fortifies it against fear.

THE END.

CPSIA information can be obtained
at www.ICGtesting.com
Printed in the USA
BVHW072143220121
598551BV00020B/141